GREAT COMPOSERS
AND THEIR MUSIC

50 Ready-to-Use Activities
for Grades 3–9

GREAT COMPOSERS AND THEIR MUSIC

50 Ready-to-Use Activities for Grades 3–9

Audrey J. Adair

Illustrated by Leah Solsrud

MUSIC CURRICULUM ACTIVITIES LIBRARY

Parker Publishing Company, Inc.
West Nyack, N.Y.

© 1987 *by*

PARKER PUBLISHING COMPANY, INC.

West Nyack, N.Y.

Library of Congress Cataloging-in-Publication Data

Adair, Audrey J.
  Great composers and their music.

  (Music curriculum activities library ; unit 5)
  1. School music—Instruction and study.   2. Music
appreciation.   I. Title.   II. Series: Adair, Audrey J.,
            Music curriculum activities library ;
unit 5.
MT10.A14   1987   unit 5   372.8'7 s [372.8'72]   87-8840

ISBN 0-13-363797-2

Printed in the United States of America

What Each Unit Offers You

A quick examination of the **Contents** will reveal a well balanced curriculum. Included are the titles of all activities, the level of difficulty, and the skill involved. The exception to this is Unit 6, where the date and special day, rather than the skill, are listed with the title of each activity.

Each of the **50 reproducible activity sheets** generally presents a single idea, with a consistent format and easy-to-follow directions on how to do the activity, along with a sufficient amount of material to enable the student to become proficient through independent and self-directed work. Because each activity has but one single behavioral objective, mastery of each skill builds confidence that allows the learner to continue progressively toward a more complete understanding of the structure of music, appreciation of music, and its uses. The activity sheets are just the right length, too, designed to be completed within a class period.

The **Progress Chart** provides a uniform, objective method of determining what skills have been mastered. With the aid of this chart, you will be able to keep track of goals, set priorities, organize daily and weekly lesson plans, and track assignments. The Progress Chart lists each activity and skill involved, and has a space for individual names or classes to be recorded and checked when each activity and skill is complete. The Progress Chart is ideal for accurate record keeping. It provides a quick, sure method for you to determine each individual student's achievements or weaknesses.

Use the **Teacher's Guide** for practical guidance on how the particular Unit will work for you. An easy effective learning system, this guide provides background information and reveals new techniques for teaching the Unit.

Throughout the *Library*, each **Answer Key** is designed with a well-thought-out system for checking students' answers. While some activities are self-checking without the use of the Answer Key, other activities can easily be student corrected, too, by simply duplicating the answer page and cutting apart the answers by activity number.

The **Self-Improvement Chart** provides the student with a self-assessment system that links curriculum goals with individual goals. By means of an appraisal checklist, the chart gives the student and teacher alike the key to finding individual talent. It also measures accountability. Included in the chart are (1) a method for recording goals and acquired music skills; (2) a log for attendance at special music events; (3) a music and instrument check-out record; (4) a log for extra credit activities and music projects; (5) a record of special music recognition awards, incentive badges, Music Share-a-Grams, Return-a-Grams; and (6) a record of music progress.

times as needed and give a copy to each student. Even paper grading can be kept to a minimum by reproducing the answer key for self-checking.

The collection of activities includes practice in classifying, matching, listing, researching, naming, drawing, decoding, identifying, doing picture or crossword puzzles, anagrams, word searches, musical word squares, and much much more.

These materials may be used successfully with students in grades 3 and up. The activities and artwork are intentionally structured to appeal to a wide range of ages. For this reason, no grade-level references appear on the activity sheets so that you can use them in a variety of classroom settings, although suggested ability levels (beginner, intermediate, advanced) appear in the Contents.

The potential uses for the *Library* for any musical purpose (or even inter-disciplinary study) are countless. Why? Because these activities allow you to in-struct an entire class, a smaller group within the classroom, or individual students. While you are actively engaged in teaching one group of students, the activity sheets may be completed by another group. In any kind of classroom setting, even with the gifted music student or the remedial child, no student needs to sit idle. Now you will have more time for individual instruction.

The Units may be used in a comprehensive music skills program, in an enrich-ment program, or even in a remedial program. The *Library* is perfect for building a comprehensive musicianship program, improving basic music skills, teaching career awareness, building music vocabulary, exploring instruments, developing good taste in listening to music, appreciating different types of music, creating a positive learning environment, and providing growing confidence in the performer.

About the Author

Audrey J. Adair has taught music at all levels in the Houston, Texas, and Dade County, Florida, public schools. She has served as a music consultant, music specialist, general music instructor, choir director, and classroom teacher. In addition, she has written a series of musical programs for assemblies and holiday events, conducted music workshops, organized music programs for the community, established glee club organizations, and done specialization work with gifted and special needs students. Currently, she directs and coordinates children's choirs, performs as soloist with flute as well as voice, and composes sacred music.

Mrs. Adair received her B.A. in Music Education from St. Olaf College in Northfield, Minnesota, and has done graduate work at the University of Houston and Florida Atlantic University in Fort Lauderdale. She is also the author of *Ready-to-Use Music Activities Kit* (Parker Publishing Company), a resource containing over 200 reproducible worksheets to teach basic music skills and concepts.

About the *Library*

The *Music Curriculum Activities Library* was developed for you, the busy classroom teacher or music specialist, to provide a variety of interesting, well-rounded, step-by-step activities ready for use in your music classroom. The *Library*'s seven carefully planned Units combine imagination, motivation, and student involvement to make learning as exciting as going on a field trip and as easy as listening to music.

The units of the *Music Curriculum Activities Library* are designed to be used separately or in conjunction with each other. Each Unit contains 50 *all new* ready-to-use music activity sheets that can be reproduced as many times as needed for use by individual students. These 350 illustrated, easy-to-read activities will turn even your most reluctant students into eager learners. Each Unit offers a wealth of information on the following topics:

Unit 1: *Basic Music Theory* develops an understanding of the basic elements of melody, rhythm, harmony, and dynamics.

Unit 2: *Reading and Writing Music* provides a source of reinforcement and instills confidence in the beginner performer through a wide range of note-reading and writing activities in the treble clef, bass clef, and in the clef of one's own instrument.

Unit 3: *Types of Musical Form and Composition* gives the student the foundation needed to enjoy worthwhile music by becoming acquainted with a wide variety of styles and representative works.

Unit 4: *Musical Instruments and the Voice* provides knowledge of and insight into the characteristic sounds of band, orchestra, folk instruments, and the voice.

Unit 5: *Great Composers and Their Music* familiarizes the student with some of the foremost composers of the past and present and their music; and cultivates an early taste for good music.

Unit 6: *Special Days Throughout the Year* offers the student well-illustrated, music-related activities that stimulate interest and discussion about music through holidays and special occasions for the entire school year.

Unit 7: *Musicians in Action* helps the student examine music as a pastime or for a career by exploring daily encounters with music and the skills, duties, environment, and requirements of a variety of careers in music.

How to Use the *Library*

     The activities in each Unit of the *Library* may be sequenced and developed in different ways. The general teacher may want to use one activity after the other, while the music specialist may prefer to use the activities in conjunction with the sequencing of the music curriculum. Teachers with special or individualized needs may select activities from various Units and use them over and over before actually introducing new material.

     Let's take a closer look at how you can use the *Music Curriculum Activities Library* in your particular classroom situation:

     . . . For THE MUSIC TEACHER who is accountable for teaching classes at many grade levels, there is a wide range of activities with varying degrees of difficulty. The activity sheets are ideal to strengthen and review skills and concepts suitable for the general music class.

     . . . For THE NEW TEACHER STARTING A GENERAL MUSIC CLASS, these fun-filled activities will provide a well-balanced, concrete core program.

     . . . For THE SPECIALIZED TEACHER who needs to set definite teaching goals, these activities offer a wealth of information about certain areas of music, such as career awareness, composers, and musical forms.

     . . . For THE BAND AND CHOIR DIRECTOR, these activity sheets are a valuable resource to explore band, orchestra, and folk instruments, along with the singing voice.

     . . . For THE PRIVATE MUSIC TEACHER who wants to sharpen and improve students' note reading skills, the *Library* offers ample homework assignments to give students the additional practice they need. There are many activity sheets using the clef of one's instrument and theory pages with illustrations of the keyboard.

     . . . For THE MUSIC CONSULTANT using any one of the units, there are plenty of activities specifically correlated to the various areas of music providing reinforcement of learning. The activity sheets are suitable for class adoption in correlation with any music book series.

     . . . For THE THEORY TEACHER, there are activities to show the students that music analysis is fun and easy.

     . . . For THE TEACHER WHO NEEDS AN ADEQUATE MEANS OF EVALUATING STUDENT PROGRESS, there are fact-filled activities ideal for diagnostic purposes. A space is provided on each sheet for a score to be given.

. . . For THE CLASSROOM TEACHER with little or no musical background, the *Library* offers effective teaching with the flexibility of the seven units. All that has to be done is to decide on the music skill or concept to be taught and then duplicate the necessary number of copies. Even the answers can be duplicated for self-checking.

. . . For THE SUBSTITUTE TEACHER, these sheets are ideal for seatwork assignments because the directions are generally self-explanatory with minimal supervision required.

. . . For THE INSTRUCTOR OF GIFTED STUDENTS, the activities may be used for any type of independent, individualized instruction and learning centers. When used in an individualized fashion, the gifted student has an opportunity to pursue music learning at his or her own pace.

. . . For THE TEACHER OF SPECIAL EDUCATION, even the disadvantaged and remedial student can get in on the fun. Each concept or skill will be mastered as any lesson may be repeated or reinforced with another activity. Some of these activity sheets are designed to provide success for students who have difficulty in other subject areas.

. . . For the INDIVIDUAL who desires to broaden and expand his or her own knowledge and interest in music, each Unit provides 50 activities to help enjoy music.

The *Music Curriculum Activities Library* is ideally a teacher's program because a minimum of planning is required. A quick glance at the Contents in each Unit reveals the titles of all the activity sheets, the ability level necessary to use them, and the skills involved for each student. Little knowledge of music is generally needed to introduce the lessons, and extensive preparation is seldom necessary. You will, of course, want to read through the activity before presenting it to the class. In cases where you need to give information about the activity, two different approaches might be considered. (1) Use the activity as a basis for a guided discussion before completing the activity to achieve the desired results, or (2) Use the activity as a foundation for a lesson plan and then follow up by completing the activity. Either one of these approaches will enhance your own and your students' confidence and, by incorporating a listening or performing experience with this directed study, the students will have a well-rounded daily lesson.

All activity sheets throughout the *Library* have the same format. They are presented in an uncluttered, easy-to-read fashion, with self-explanatory directions. You need no extra materials or equipment, except for an occasional pair of scissors. The classroom or resource area should, however, contain a few reference books, such as song books or music series' books, encyclopedias, reference books about composers, a dictionary, music dictionary or glossary, and so on, so that while working on certain activities the student has easy access to resource books. Then, you simply need to duplicate the activity sheet as many

These specific features of the chart will help you:

- Provide a uniform, objective method of determining rewards for students.
- Assess future curriculum needs by organizing long-term information on student performance.
- Foster understanding of why students did or did not qualify for additional merit.
- Motivate students by giving them feedback on ways for self-improvement.
- Assist students in making statements of their own desires and intentions for learning, and in checking progress toward their goals.

The **Music Share-a-Gram** is a personalized progress report addressed to the parent and created to show the unique qualities of the individual child. It allows you to pinpoint areas of success and tell parents what they need to know about their child. The Music Share-a-Gram evaluates twelve important abilities and personal traits with ratings from exceptional to unsatisfactory, which you might want to discuss with students to solicit their reaction. For example, you might use these ratings as a basis for selecting a student to attend the gifted program in music. This form is designed to be sent with or without the Return-a-Gram, and may be hand-delivered by the student or sent through the mail. For easy record keeping, make a copy of the Gram and attach it to the back of the Student Record Profile Chart.

The **Return-a-Gram** is designed to accompany the Music Share-a-Gram and is sent to the parent on special occasions. When a reply is not expected or necessary, simply detach the Return-a-Gram before sending the Share-a-Gram. This form encourages feedback from the parent and even allows the parent to arrange for a parent-teacher conference. Both Grams are printed on the same page and are self-explanatory—complete with a dotted line for the parent to detach, fill in, and return.

The **Student Record Profile Chart** is a guide for understanding and helping students, and offers a means of periodic evaluation. The chart is easy to use and provides all you need for accurate record keeping and measuring accountability for individual student progress throughout all seven units. It provides an accumulative skills profile for the student and represents an actual score of his or her written performance for each activity. Here is a workable form that you can immediately tailor to your own requirements for interpretation and use of scores. Included are clear instructions, with an example, to help you record your students' assessment on a day-to-day basis, to keep track of pupil progress, and to check learning patterns over a period of time. This chart allows you to spot the potential superior achiever along with the remedial individual. The chart coordinates all aspects of data ranging from the students' name, class, school, classroom teacher's name, semester, date, page number, actual grade, and attendance.

The **Word List** is presented as a reinforcement for building a music vocabulary. It emphasizes the use of dictionary skills; the students make a glossary of important words related to the particular unit. Its purpose is to encourage the use of vocabulary skills by helping develop an understanding of the music terms, concepts, and names found on the activity sheets. This vocabulary reference page is meant to be reproduced and used by the individual student throughout the units as a guide for spelling, word recognition, pronunciation, recording definitions, plus any other valuable information. Throughout six units of the *Library*, a cumulation of the words are presented on the Word List pages. (A Word List is not included in Unit 6.) With the help of this extensive vocabulary, when the student uses the words on both the activity page and the Word List, they will become embedded as part of his or her language.

Each Unit contains a wide-ranging collection of **Incentive Badges**. Use them to reward excellence, commend effort, for bonuses, prizes, behavior modification, or as reminders. These badges are designed to capture the interest and attention of the entire school. Several badges are designed with an open-ended format to provide maximum flexibility in meeting any special music teaching requirement.

Included in each Unit is a simple **Craft Project** that may be created by the entire class or by individual students. Each craft project is an integral part of the subject matter of that particular unit and will add a rich dimension to the activities. The materials necessary for the construction of the craft projects have been limited to those readily available in most classrooms and call for no special technical or artistic skills.

PLUS each Unit contains:

- Worked-out sample problems for students to use as a standard and model for their own work.

- Additional teaching suggestions in the Answer Key for getting the most out of certain activities.

- Extra staff paper for unlimited use, such as composing, ear training, improvising, or writing chords.

- Activities arranged in a sequential pattern.

Resources for Teaching Music More Effectively

- Have a classroom dictionary available for reference.
- Have a glossary or music dictionary available for reference.
- Use only one activity sheet per class session.
- Distribute the Word List prior to the first activity sheet of the particular unit. Encourage students to underline familiar words on the list and write definitions or identifications on the back before instruction on the unit begins. Later, the students can compare their answers with those studied.
- Provide short-term goals for each class session and inform students in advance that awards will be given for the day. You'll see how their conduct improves, too.
- Encourage students to make or buy an inexpensive folder to store music activity sheets, craft projects, word lists, self-evaluation charts, and so on. Folders might be kept in the classroom when not in use and distributed at the beginning of each class period.
- Many of the activities are ideal for bulletin board display. If space is not available to display all students' work, rotate the exhibits.
- Encourage students to re-read creative writing pages for clarity and accuracy before copying the final form on the activity sheet. Proofreading for grammatical and spelling errors should be encouraged.
- For creative drawing activities, encourage students to sketch their initial ideas on another sheet of paper first, then draw the finished product on the activity sheet. It is not necessary to have any technical ability in drawing to experience the pleasure of these creative activities.
- Although you will probably want to work through parts of some activities with your students, and choose some activities for group projects, you will find that most lessons are designed to lead students to the correct answers with little or no teacher direction. Students can be directed occasionally to work through an activity with a partner to search out and correct specific errors.
- Self-corrections and self-checking make a much better impression on young learners than do red-penciled corrections by the classroom music teacher.
- On activities where answers will vary, encourage students to rate their own work on correctness, originality, completeness, carefulness, realism, and organization.

• Most activity pages will serve as a "teacher assistant" in developing specific skills or subject areas to study. The activities throughout the series are complete with learning objectives and are generally factual enough for the teacher to use as a basis for a daily lesson plan.

• The library research activities promote creativity instead of copying while students search out relevant data from a variety of sources, such as encyclopedias, dictionaries, reference books, autobiographies, and others. These activities are ideal for the individual student or groups of students working beyond the classroom environment.

• The following are practical guidelines in planning, organizing, and constructing the Craft Projects:

. . . Acquaint yourself with any of the techniques that are new to you before you ask your students to undertake the project.

. . . Decide on your project and assemble the materials before you begin.

. . . Make a sample model for experience.

. . . Use a flat surface for working.

. . . Be sure the paper is cut exactly to measurements and that folds are straight.

. . . Be available for consultation.

. . . Provide guidance on what the next logical step is to encourage all students to finish their projects.

. . . Use the finished craft projects as displays and points of interest for your school's open house.

• Many of the Incentive Badges found in each Unit are open-ended and can be made effective communication tools to meet your needs. Extra space is provided on these badges for additional written messages that might be used for any number of reasons. Be creative for your own special needs; load the copier with colored paper and print as many as you need for the semester or entire school year. Then simply use a paper cutter to separate the badges and sort them out alphabetically. Make an alphabetical index on file card dividers using these titles. Next, arrange them in an accessible file box or shoe box, depending on the size needed. Include a roll of tape to attach the badge to the recipient.

Teacher's Guide to Unit 5

Great Composers and Their Music will help your students relate to the composer, stimulate music listening and performance in the classroom, and provide a creative responsiveness in each child.

Divided into five distinct parts, Unit 5 is designed to teach many different things. The creative drawing section is related to your students' own musical experiences. Always encourage students to do original artwork, and gear the activity toward what you are studying (popular, classical, and so on). Activities 5–5 through 5–10 are designed to go hand-in-hand with listening experiences. Most schools will have these standard numbers in their music record library; if not, the local library or even your own personal library might be other sources to consider.

The second part, "Creative Writing," is designed to teach a love and understanding for music by having your students learn more about the composers who wrote the music. Again, use these activities in conjunction with the music being studied. Encourage students to work on scrap paper first, then recopy the final draft on the activity sheet.

The next section on the masters and their works provides an incentive for you in presenting lessons on composers and their works. For example, while listening to different dances from various periods in history, let the activity "Dance Data" be your guide for teaching a series of lessons. Then introduce an example from each period. Conclude by using the activity as a follow-up exercise for the class.

The section, "A Closer Look at Some Famous Classical Composers," examines the lives and music of six famous masters. A way of introducing one of these activities might be to select a composer of the week. Then use the corresponding activity as a lesson guide and complete the activity sheet at the end of the week's study. During class periods, provide several listening experiences, hold animated discussions, and use other activity sheets for continuity. For example, Activity 5–15 is a perfect complementary activity while studying the life of any composer. Assign the more able students in class outside listening or reading. Construct a collective scrapbook and post any related items on the bulletin board. Encourage students to keep a music notebook with a record of music heard in class and a few comments about the composition. Include the composer's name, nationality, and some interesting facts about his life.

The final part of Unit 5 is a rich assortment of activities for the entire class, small groups within the classroom, or for individual students doing independent study. Many of the activities, like "Get to Know Sousa," can be used as a basis for your lesson plan and may be completed by the entire class after a lively discussion and a related listening experience. Most activities can be completed within the classroom, while some need special resource information. "Who, What, and When," for example, might best be suited for library research. A quick look at the activity page will tell you if it lends itself to your particular classroom situation.

The activities in Unit 5 should be used in conjunction with a listening or performing experience; they are *not* intended to be used as busywork.

Contents

Activity Number/Title	Skill Involved	Level of Difficulty
Creative Drawing		
5-1 DESIGNER'S WORKSHOP	Drawing a portrait or caricature of a composer and writing a slogan	Beginner
5-2 MY FAVORITE SONG IS . . .	Drawing a picture describing a favorite song with the composer's name	Beginner
5-3 AN AUTHENTIC PORTRAIT	Sketching a picture of a favorite composer	Beginner
5-4 SHOW AND TELL	Designing a record album jacket for a favorite song	Beginner
5-5 PETER AND THE WOLF	Drawing characters to match the sounds of the instruments	Beginner
5-6 CARNIVAL OF THE ANIMALS	Drawing animals to match the sounds of instruments	Beginner
5-7 THE NUTCRACKER SUITE	Illustrating the handsome prince	Beginner
5-8 SCHEHERAZADE	Drawing the Sultan or Sultana Scheherazade	Beginner
5-9 THE SORCERER'S APPRENTICE	Drawing one of the scenes from this musical story	Beginner
5-10 PICTURES AT AN EXHIBITION	Drawing a favorite picture from this symphonic work	Intermediate
Creative Writing		
5-11 A DAY IN THE LIFE OF . . .	Writing about a typical day in the life of a favorite composer	Beginner
5-12 WRITE A FEATURE STORY	Writing a feature story for the school newspaper about a composer	Beginner

Activity Number/Title	Skill Involved	Level of Difficulty
5-13 A COMPOSER'S CHOICE	Answering questions about how a composer creates, makes choices, and so on	Beginner
5-14 MY FAVORITE COMPOSER TODAY IS . . .	Writing an article about a favorite composer	Intermediate
5-15 GETTING ACQUAINTED	Gathering information about a composer	Intermediate
5-16 A PERSONAL HISTORY OF . . .	Using a guideline to write a personal history of a composer	Intermediate

Learning About the Masters and Their Works

5-17 CURTAIN CALL	Pronouncing and spelling names correctly of famous composers	Beginner
5-18 DECODE WITH VOWELS	Completing the titles of works by national composers using vowels	Beginner
5-19 WHAT'S THEIR NATIONALITY?	Writing nationalities of the masters in a crossword puzzle	Beginner and Intermediate
5-20 WHO WROTE THE OPERA?	Naming composers of famous operas	Beginner and Intermediate
5-21 CRAZY CLUES	Using crazy clues to name famous compositions	Beginner and Intermediate
5-22 COMPOSER TRIVIA	Reading statements about composers to guess their names	Beginner and Intermediate
5-23 DANCE DATA	Unscrambling and decoding names of composers who wrote famous dances	Intermediate
5-24 NAME THE OTHER TITLE	Naming another title for a symphonic work	Intermediate
5-25 WHO WROTE IT?	Naming famous composers from their works	Intermediate
5-26 COMPLETE THE TITLE	Finishing titles of famous works by the masters	Intermediate
5-27 IDENTIFY THE SYMPHONY	Identifying symphonies by clues about composers	Advanced
5-28 REVEAL THE COMPOSER	Identifying composers by clues	Advanced

A Closer Look at Some Famous Classical Composers

5-29 CLASSICAL CORNER: JOHANN SEBASTIAN BACH	Using letter names of organ pedals to complete statements about Bach	Beginner

Activity Number/Title		Skill Involved	Level of Difficulty
5–46	FINISH THE TITLE	Completing song titles of well-known composers	Intermediate
5–47	WHO, WHAT, AND WHEN?	Matching events in history to birthdates of famous composers	Advanced
5–48	MATCH THE PUZZLE PIECES	Matching composers to their operettas, musicals, or pop music	Advanced
5–49	WHEN DID THEY COMPOSE?	Matching dates in history with names of famous composers	Advanced
5–50	FINISH THE TIME LINE	Matching dates of musical highlights with literary achievements	Advanced

Activities for
CREATIVE DRAWING

Name _____   Score _____

Date _____   Class _____

DESIGNER'S WORKSHOP   5–1

Use your talent to design the front of this shirt. Draw a caricature to represent a composer or sketch a portrait of a composer. Then write an original slogan or catchy phrase to go with it; for example, "Beethoven Is Best."

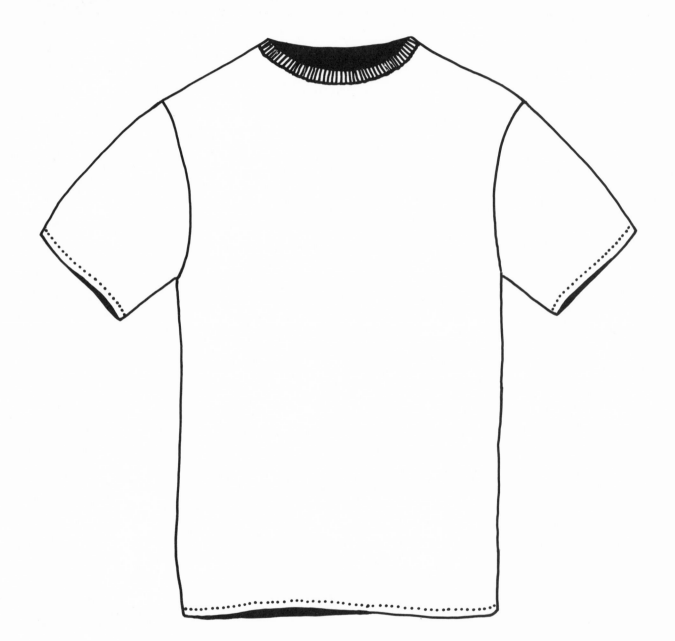

Name _____   Score _____

Date _____   Class _____

MY FAVORITE SONG IS ...   5–2

Draw a picture to describe your favorite piece of music. Be sure to include the song title, composer, and your name.

_____
Song Title

_____   _____
Drawn by   Composer's Name

Name _____   Score _____

Date _____   Class _____

AN AUTHENTIC PORTRAIT   5–3

Draw a picture of your favorite composer. Make your sketch as large as the frame and remember to sign your drawing at the bottom right-hand corner.

_____
Composer's Name

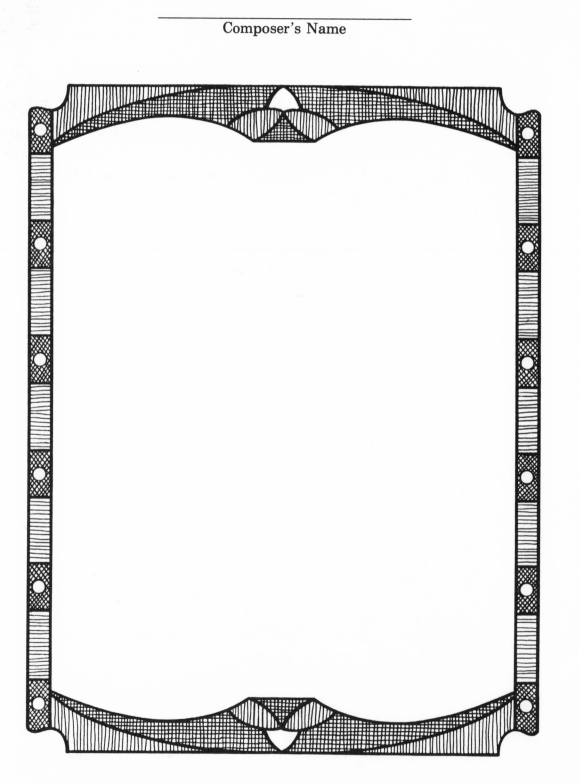

Name _____   Score _____

Date _____   Class _____

SHOW AND TELL   5–4

Design a record album jacket for a song you like best. List the composer and the title of the song.

Name _____   Score _____

Date _____   Class _____

PETER AND THE WOLF   5–5

These instruments are featured in *Peter and the Wolf* by Prokofiev. In this orchestral fairy tale, the characters are represented by different instruments. Draw the characters to match the instruments. Make your selection from the answers at the left.

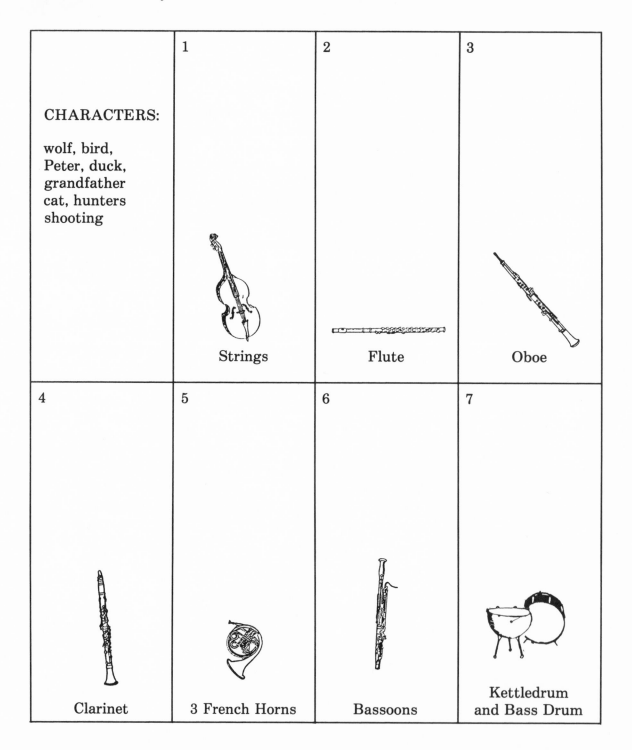

CHARACTERS:

wolf, bird,
Peter, duck,
grandfather
cat, hunters
shooting

1 Strings

2 Flute

3 Oboe

4 Clarinet

5 3 French Horns

6 Bassoons

7 Kettledrum and Bass Drum

Name _____   Score _____

Date _____   Class _____

CARNIVAL OF THE ANIMALS   5–6

In the program music *Carnival of the Animals* by Saint-Saëns, instruments are used to imitate animal sounds. In the boxes below, draw the animals to match the instruments. Choose your answers from the list. The boxes are in the order the music is played.

Elephant	Aquarium
Swan	Kangaroos
Royal March of the Lion	Turtles (Tortoises)
Pianist	Cuckoo
Fossils	Aviary
Mules	Donkeys (Personages with long ears)
Hens and Roosters	Finale (Several of the musical animals)

1	2	3	4	5
piano	piano, strings, and clarinet	two pianos	strings	double bass
6	**7**	**8**	**9**	**10**
two pianos	glockenspiel, flute, and violin	violins	clarinet and piano	flute
11	**12**	**13**	**14**	
piano	a variety of instruments	cello	a variety of instruments	

THE NUTCRACKER SUITE   5–7

Listen to *The Nutcracker* Suite by Tchaikovsky. Then draw a picture of how the nutcracker looked as a handsome prince in the girl's dream.

Name _____   Score _____

Date _____   Class _____

SCHEHERAZADE   5–8

Draw what you think either the Sultan or Sultana Scheherazade looks like from the suite, *Scheherazade*, by Rimsky-Korsakov. Make your drawing as large as the frame and sign it in the lower right-hand corner.

Name _____   Score _____

Date _____   Class _____

THE SORCERER'S APPRENTICE   5–9

Read the story of *The Sorcerer's Apprentice* and listen to the music. Then draw one of the scenes from this musical story by Dukas.

PICTURES AT AN EXHIBITION 5–10

Draw one of the pictures Mussorgsky was describing in his suite *Pictures at an Exhibition*. Be sure to make your drawing as large as the frame.

Activities for
CREATIVE WRITING

A DAY IN THE LIFE OF ...   5-11

Write a story about what you think might have been a typical day in the life of one of your favorite composers. Use the back of this sheet if you need more space to write.

A DAY IN THE LIFE OF _____

by _____

_____

_____

_____

_____

_____

_____

_____

_____

_____

_____

_____

_____

_____

_____

_____

_____

_____

_____

_____

_____

_____

_____

WRITE A FEATURE STORY   5–12

Write a short story for your school newspaper featuring a composer of your choice.

SCHOOL NEWS

_____

_____

_____

_____

_____

_____

_____

_____

A COMPOSER'S CHOICE   5–13

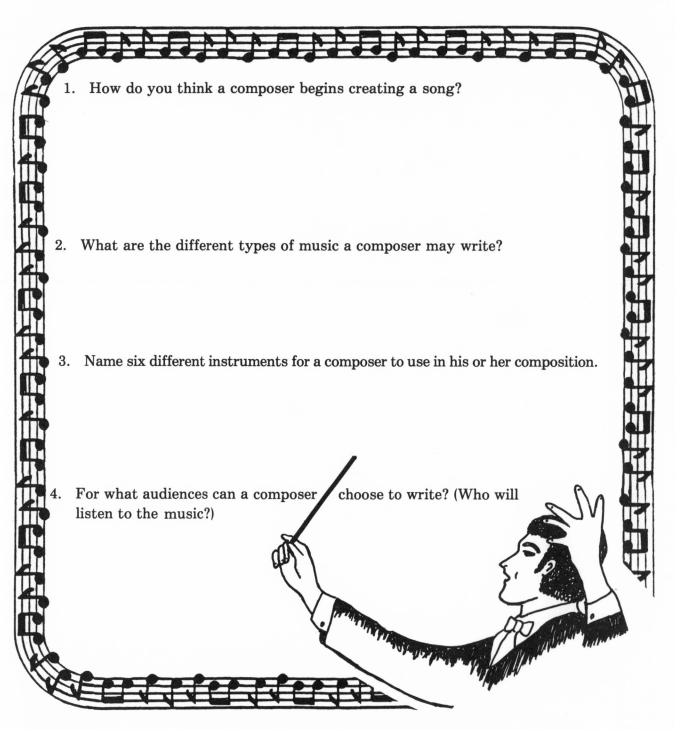

1. How do you think a composer begins creating a song?

2. What are the different types of music a composer may write?

3. Name six different instruments for a composer to use in his or her composition.

4. For what audiences can a composer choose to write? (Who will listen to the music?)

MY FAVORITE COMPOSER TODAY IS ...   5-14

Write an article about a composer whose work you like. Include what type of music he or she writes, the titles of a few works, a brief personal history, some interesting facts, and why you like this contemporary composer. Use the back of this sheet if you need more space to write.

From the desk of _____

                              Your Name

_____

_____

_____

_____

_____

_____

_____

_____

_____

_____

_____

_____

_____

_____

_____

_____

GETTING ACQUAINTED   5-15

Select a composer who lived before your time and complete the information below.

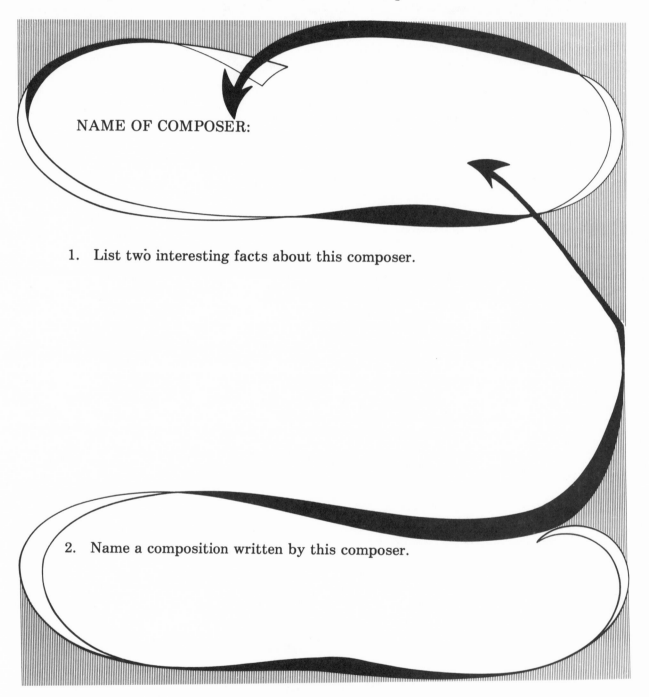

NAME OF COMPOSER:

1. List two interesting facts about this composer.

2. Name a composition written by this composer.

Name _____   Score _____

Date _____   Class _____

A PERSONAL HISTORY OF ...   5–16

Write a personal history of a composer of your choice. Include information regarding what type of a childhood the composer had; what type of music did he or she compose; in what period in history did the composer live; and interesting facts about his or her life. List your resources on the back of this page (title of book(s), author, publisher, copyright date, and the number of pages). Use another sheet of paper if you need more space to write the personal history.

Composer's Name
_____
_____
_____
_____
_____
_____
_____
_____
_____
_____
_____
_____
_____
_____
_____
_____

Activities for
LEARNING ABOUT THE MASTERS
AND THEIR WORKS

Name _____   Score _____

Date _____   Class _____

CURTAIN CALL   5–17

Imagine that you have been asked to audition for a special musical program. Try out for the part by pronouncing the names of these twenty world-famous composers. You'll pass the audition if you can match the composers' names with pronunciations below. Write the names of the composers by the correct pronunciation. Choose your answers from the list on the right to be sure your spelling is correct.

1. bahk _____

2. BAY toh vun _____

3. br AHms _____

4. show PAN _____

5. duh byoo SEE _____

6. HAN d'l _____

7. HIGH dn _____

8. HIN duh mit _____

9. list _____

10. mee YOH _____

11. MOH tsahrt _____

12. moo SAWRG skih _____

13. pro KOH fee ef _____

14. san SAHNS _____

15. SHOO bert _____

16. SHOO mahn _____

17. sha stah KOH vitch _____

18. sih BAY lih us _____

19. SOO zah _____

20. chye KAWF skih _____

Brahms
Chopin
Bach
Debussy
Beethoven
Liszt
Milhaud
Haydn
Handel
Hindemith
Mussorgsky
Prokofiev
Mozart
Schubert
Saint-Saëns
Schumann
Sousa
Tchaikovsky
Sibelius
Shostakovich

© 1981 by Parker Publishing Company, Inc.

Name _____   Score _____

Date _____   Class _____

DECODE WITH VOWELS   5–18

Below are the names of several national composers and their works. The missing letters in the titles are all vowels (A–E–I–O–U). Try to figure out what vowel is missing and write that letter on the blank to complete the title. Then check your answers by looking at the vowel code. (Vowels that begin or end a word are given.)

1. App __ l __ ch __ __ n Spr __ ng by Copland
        %   %   * %   *

2. An Am __ r __ c __ n in P __ r __ s by Gershwin
           ¢   *   %   %   *

3. Gr __ nd C __ ny __ n S __ __ te by Grofé
       %   %   %   + *

4. N __ w W __ rld Symph __ ny by Dvořák
       *   #   #

5. B __ lg __ r __ __ n D __ nc __ s by Bartók
       +   %   * %   %   ¢

6. H.M.S. P __ n __ f __ re by Gilbert and Sullivan
               *   %   #

7. Symph __ ny No. 2 (L __ nd __ n) by Vaughan Williams
           #   #   #

8. F __ nl __ nd __ a by Sibelius
       *   %   *

9. H __ ng __ r __ __ n D __ nc __ s by Brahms
       +   %   * %   %   ¢

10. Isr __ __ l Symph __ ny by Bloch
         %   ¢   #

11. N __ rw __ g __ __ n D __ nc __ s by Grieg
       #   ¢   * %   %   ¢

12. 1812 Ov __ rt __ re by Tchaikovsky
              ¢   +

VOWEL CODE:

A   E   I   O   U
%   ¢   *   #   +

WHAT'S THEIR NATIONALITY?   5–19

Here's a puzzle for those of you who like geography. All of these famous composers are from different countries. Write their nationalities in the puzzle.

ACROSS

4. Liszt
5. Elgar
8. Grieg
10. Smetana and Dvořák
11. Sibelius
12. Granados

DOWN

1. Wagner and Beethoven
2. Chopin
3. Tchaikovsky
6. Verdi
7. Debussy
9. Copland

WHO WROTE THE OPERA?   5-20

Listed here are the names of famous operas, folk operas, and operettas. Write the composer's name in the puzzle, choosing your answers from the list at the bottom of the sheet. The first one has been done for you.

ACROSS

3. *Tannhauser*
5. *Porgy and Bess*
8. *Amahl and the Night Visitors*
9. *The Student Prince*
12. *Madame Butterfly*
13. *Carmen*
14. *The Magic Flute*

DOWN

1. *The Merry Widow*
2. *Aida*
4. *The Mikado* by Gilbert and _____
6. *Hansel and Gretel*
7. *Martha*
10. *William Tell*
11. *Tales of Hoffman*

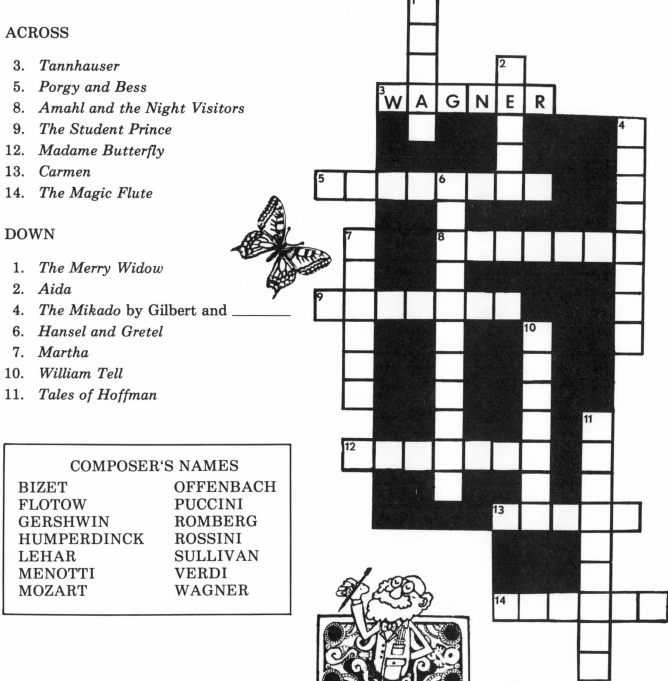

```
COMPOSER'S NAMES
BIZET           OFFENBACH
FLOTOW          PUCCINI
GERSHWIN        ROMBERG
HUMPERDINCK     ROSSINI
LEHAR           SULLIVAN
MENOTTI         VERDI
MOZART          WAGNER
```

Name _____      Score _____

Date _____   Class _____

CRAZY CLUES   5–21

First fold the bottom part of this page back to hide the answers. Name the famous compositions by reading the crazy clues. Then look at the composer's name for a final clue. See how many questions you can answer on your own.

1. This sonata may remind you of looking at the moon. _____

   _____ by Ludwig van Beethoven

2. This musical has nothing to do with the east side of town. _____

   _____ by Leonard Bernstein

3. You may be reminded of this opera when eating oysters. _____

   _____ by Georges Bizet

4. This composition, first performed as a ballet, but known today as an orchestra suite is not

   "Springtime in the Rockies." _____

   _____ by Aaron Copland

5. The magician in this composition has no rabbits in his hat. _____

   _____ by Paul Dukas

6. The visitors in this opera did not include Santa Claus. _____

   _____ by Gian-Carlo Menotti

7. This fairy tale for a narrator and orchestra does not mention the three little pigs or a

   famous rabbit, but has a boy by the rabbit's name. _____

   _____ by Serge Prokofiev

8. By reading the title of this ballet, one might think it's about nuts and crackers. _____

   _____ by Peter Ilich Tchaikovsky

- -

Check your answers: 1. Moonlight Sonata   2. West Side Story   3. The Pearl Fishers
4. Appalachian Spring   5. The Sorcerer's Apprentice   6. Amahl and the Night Visitors
7. Peter and the Wolf   8. The Nutcracker

COMPOSER TRIVIA 5–22

How good are you at composer trivia? Read the statements below and try to guess the composer's name. Then check your answers and make any corrections by using the answers in order at the bottom.

1. _____ He composed with incredible speed. He completed one movement of a quartet in less than five hours. Sometimes he wrote six or eight songs a day.

2. _____ He wrote two harpsichord minuets at the age of five.

3. _____ As an infant a beautiful tone made his face shine while discord brought an expression of pain. He was taught to play the piano at age two and a half.

4. _____ He and his music were more or less forgotten soon after his death.

5. _____ Stone-deaf, he continued conducting the orchestra after the symphony ended.

6. _____ At the age of twelve he was dismissed as organist because he refused to hold a fermata that was not indicated in the music.

7. _____ His annual income went into the six figures.

8. _____ He is considered a national hero in Norway.

9. _____ He often worked sixteen hours a day and usually on several compositions at one time.

10. _____ Strange fears obsessed him. While conducting an orchestra, he feared his head might slip off his shoulders so he held up his chin with his left hand.

Franz Schubert
Wolfgang Amadeus Mozart
Camille Saint-Saëns
Johann Sebastian Bach
Ludwig van Beethoven
Samuel Barber
George Gershwin
Edvard Grieg
Joseph Haydn
Peter Ilich Tchaikovsky

DANCE DATA   5-23

Listed below by century are the names of famous dances and the scrambled names of the composers who wrote these famous compositions. See how many names you can unscramble without looking at the number key at the bottom of the page. After you have written the names of all the composers, look at the list of dances again. Circle the names of any dances you have heard.

Baroque Dances:

1. English Suite No. 2 in A Minor (Allemande, Courante, Sarabande, Bourrée, Gigue)

   by CHAB _____
   25 26 24 19

2. Suite No. 5 in E Major (Allemande, Courante) by DLENAH _____
   19 26 15 23 22 15

Eighteenth-Century Minuets:

3. *Don Giovanni,* Minuet in Act 1 by RATMOZ _____
   14 12 1 26 9 7

4. String Quartet in C Major "Emperor" by HANDY _____
   19 26 2 23 13

Nineteenth-Century Dances:

5. *The Nutcracker* Suite "Waltz of the Flowers"

   by SVKYOKCHATI _____
   7 24 19 26 18 16 12 5 8 16 2

6. Polonaise by CHINOP _____
   24 19 12 11 18 13

7. *Liebeslieder* Waltzes by AMSBRH _____
   25 9 26 19 14 8

Twentieth-Century Dances:

8. Bolero by LEVAR _____
   9 26 5 22 15

9. Three Preludes for Piano by WINSHERG _____
   20 22 9 8 19 4 18 13

10. *Children's Corner Suite* "Golliwog's Cake Walk" by SEDBUSY

    _____
    23 22 25 6 8 8 2

A	B	C	D	E	F	G	H	I	J	K	L	M
26	25	24	23	22	21	20	19	18	17	16	15	14

N	O	P	Q	R	S	T	U	V	W	X	Y	Z
13	12	11	10	9	8	7	6	5	4	3	2	1

Name _____   Score _____

Date _____   Class _____

NAME THE OTHER TITLE   5-24

Each of these composers wrote symphonies known by two different titles. One title is given. Write the other well-known title in the puzzle. Figure out as many titles as you can on your own before looking at the answers printed upside down at the bottom of the page.

ACROSS

3. MENDELSSOHN
   Symphony No. 4 in A Major

5. SHOSTAKOVICH
   Symphony No. 7

6. BEETHOVEN
   Symphony No. 3 in E-flat Major

7. MOZART
   Symphony No. 41 in C Major, K551

10. DVORAK
    Symphony No. 5 in E minor

11. HAYDN
    Symphony No. 101 in D Major

DOWN

1. SCHUBERT
   Symphony No. 8 in B minor

2. TCHAIKOVSKY
   Symphony No. 6 in B minor, Op. 74

4. HAYDN
   Symphony No. 94 in G Major

8. BEETHOVEN
   Symphony No. 6 in F Major

9. SCHUMANN
   Symphony No. 3 in E-flat Major

ANSWERS

Across
3. Italian
5. Leningrad
6. Eroica
7. Jupiter
10. World
11. Clock

Down
1. Unfinished
2. Pathétique
4. Surprise
8. Pastorale
9. Rhenish

WHO WROTE IT?   5-25

Below are the scrambled names of nine famous composers. Look at the compositions they wrote to unscramble their names. Then write their names in the puzzle.

ACROSS

_HENDLA_____   2. The Messiah

_STAIN-SNASË_____   4. Carnival of the Animals

_CHAB_____   6. Mass in B Minor

_PROOFIVEK_____   9. Lieutenant Kije Suite

DOWN

_LOPCAND_____   1. Billy the Kid

_SADUK_____   3. The Sorcerer's Apprentice

_CHIKOYSKVAT_____   5. The Nutcracker

_WERGNISH_____   7. An American in Paris

_LEVAR_____   8. Bolero

COMPLETE THE TITLE

Complete the titles of these works written by the following composers. Then write the words in the puzzle.

ACROSS

1. A Midsummer Night's
   D _ _ _ M
   by Mendelssohn

4. Pictures at an
   E _ _ _ _ _ _ _ _ N
   by Mussorgsky

6. The Sorcerer's
   A _ _ _ _ _ _ _ _ E
   by Dukas

7. Water M _ _ _ C
   by Handel

8. Prelude to the Afternoon of a
   F _ _ N by Debussy

11. Sleeping B _ _ _ _ Y
    by Tchaikovsky

12. Swan L _ _ E by Tchaikovsky

13. Peter and the W _ _ F
    by Prokofiev

DOWN

2. Carnival of the A _ _ _ _ _ S
   by Saint-Saëns

3. Night on Bald M _ _ _ _ _ _ N
   by Mussorgsky

5. The Fountains of R _ _ E by Respighi

9. Grand Canyon S _ _ _ E by Grofé

10. Prelude to Hansel and G _ _ _ _ L
    by Humperdinck

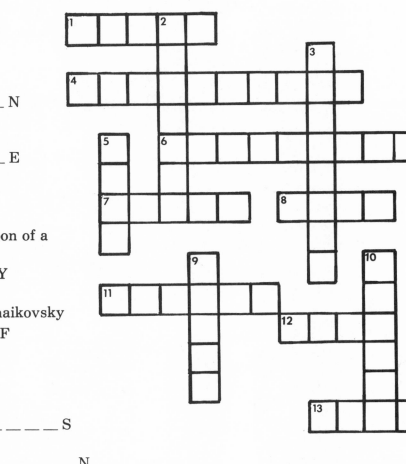

IDENTIFY THE SYMPHONY

5–27

Each clue gives the composer's name and tells something about the symphony that makes it unique.

ACROSS

1. Haydn—It has a big drum crash.

5. This is one of Mendelssohn's most frequently played symphonies.

7. Shostakovich—Reflects the feelings of the time of a great Russian city.

10. Beethoven—Usually known by its Italian name; it was written to honor Napoleon.

13. Beethoven—A storm occurs.

14. Haydn—It has the imitation of a tick-tock beat.

15. Ralph Vaughan Williams—The street noises of the British capital are worked in.

DOWN

2. Schubert's most famous work; for unknown reasons was never completed.

3. Tchaikovsky introduced a theme from the Russian "Mass for the Dead."

4. Beethoven used a chord combining all seven steps of the d minor scale.

6. Dvořák is greatest in slow movements such as the "Largo" movement of the "New _____ Symphony."

8. Haydn, or as historians now believe, Mozart's father, Leopold, wrote this for children using the sound of a toy trumpet, a rattle, and a cuckoo whistle.

9. Haydn—Toward the end the musicians leave one after the other.

11. The composer, Prokofiev, tries some experimental ideas.

12. One of Mozart's most famous symphonies— it has delicate beauty, pleasing to the ear.

Name _____   Score _____

Date _____   Class _____

REVEAL THE COMPOSER

ACROSS

2. A great composer who wrote music especially for the piano.

3. Johann _____, the composer of "The Beautiful Blue Danube."

5. A great composer of orchestral music who became deaf in later years.

7. A Norwegian composer who wrote music for Henrik Ibsen's play, *Peer Gynt*.

8. A Bohemian Composer who wrote the popular "Humoresque."

10. A Hungarian composer, who earned the title, "King of Pianists."

11. A great French composer who wrote the piano piece, "Clair de lune."

13. A German composer who wrote the opera, *Hansel and Gretel*.

16. A French composer who introduced animal sounds in *The Carnival of the Animals*.

17. The first to write a large number of symphonies.

18. *The Sorcerer's Apprentice* made him world famous.

DOWN

1. _____, the greatest child prodigy in music, was a genius of a composer.

4. Franz _____ wrote the operetta, *The Merry Widow*.

6. This composer's most famous work is his oratorio, The *Messiah*.

9. Rimsky-_____ wrote a piece about a flight of a bumblebee.

12. He was known as the last of the "Three B's," Bach, Beethoven and _____.

14. _____, born in 1685, was a musical genius and the founder of musical science.

15. _____ was an Italian composer and is well-known for his operas, *La Traviata, Aida, Rigoletto, Othello,* and *Falstaff*.

Activities for
A CLOSER LOOK AT
SOME FAMOUS CLASSICAL COMPOSERS

CLASSICAL CORNER: JOHANN SEBASTIAN BACH   5-29

The last words in each of these statements about Johann Sebastian Bach are missing one or more letters. These words may be completed by using any of the letters from the organ pedals below.

1. Bach was a German __ ompos __ r.

2. Bach never thought of himself as a genius; however, his works filled sixty volum __ s.

3. At the age of nine Bach copied an entire music library by moonlight and almost ruined his

   __ y __ si __ ht.

4. Bach was a humble and deeply religious man. He lived to serve God and write music primarily for the __ hur __ h.

5. His three most famous works for the church are: Mass in B minor, "The Passion According to St. John," and "The Passion According to St. M __ tth __ w."

6. Bach wrote around three hundred cantatas for the church. These works, based on scripture, were written for the voi __ __.

7. The music Bach wrote for the Well-Tempered Clavier is today played on the pi __ no.

8. Bach's famous Toccata and Fugue in D minor was written for the or __ __ n.

9. Bach wrote his Brandenburg concertos for solo instrument and or __ h __ str __ .

10. The death of Bach in 1750 marked the end of the Baroque P __ rio __ .

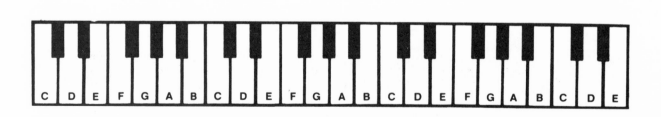

CLASSICAL CORNER: GEORGE FREDERICK HANDEL   5-30

Try to complete as many missing words below before looking at the mirrored answers at the bottom of the page.

1. George Frederick Handel began

   _ _ _ _ _ _ _ _ _ when he was only ten years old.

2. George Frederick learned a great deal about compo-

   sition by _ _ _ _ _ _ _ works from the old masters.

3. To fulfill his father's wish, Handel studied _ _ _ until he was seventeen.

4. It is not as a composer of operas, sonatas, orchestra music, or piano music that we remember Handel. It

   is for the *Messiah* that his _ _ _ _ will live forever.

5. The *Messiah*, written in 1741, is the greatest oratorio ever _ _ _ _ _ _ _ _ _.

6. An oratorio is a work for solo voices, chorus and orchestra with the _ _ _ _ _ adapted from the Bible.

7. It took Handel less than a _ _ _ _ _ _ to compose the *Messiah*, and during this time he appeared to be in some type of trance.

8. When Handel's *Messiah* was first performed in London, the king stood with a bowed head for the "Hallelujah Chorus." Since that time it has become a custom for audiences to _ _ _ _ when the "Hallelujah Chorus" is sung.

9. During the last seven years of his life, Handel was _ _ _ _ _ _. He would dictate his music as someone would write it down.

10. There is a statue of George Frederick Handel in the poets' corner in Westminster Abbey. Beside the marble statue is a table with a carved sheet of music from _ _ _

    _ _ _ _ _ _.

1. COMPOSING   2. COPYING   3. LAW   4. NAME   5. COMPOSED
6. TEXT   7. MONTH   8. RISE   9. BLIND   10. THE MESSIAH

CLASSICAL CORNER: WOLFGANG AMADEUS MOZART   5-31

Can you decode the words below to complete each statement about Mozart? Here are two clues to help you figure out the numerical code:

20 = G   14 = M

1. Mozart had exceptional musical gifts and was a musical __ __ __ __ __ __ .
    20 22 13 18 6 8

2. At the age of five, Mozart composed two __ __ __ __ __ __ __ for the harpsichord.
    14 18 13 6 22 7 8

3. Mozart wrote a complete sonata when he was seven years old and composed a

    __ __ __ __ __ __ __ __ when he was eight.
    8 2 14 11 19 12 30 2

4. One of Mozart's greatest Italian operas was *The* __ __ __ __ __ __ __ __ *of Figaro.*
    14 26 9 9 18 26 20 22

5. Mozart had an extraordinary __ __ __ __ __ __ , and after hearing a melody once, he could
    14 22 14 12 9 2

    reproduce it without error.

6. When blindfolded he could identify

    __ __ __ __ __ and chords.
    7 12 13 22 8

7. Given a theme Mozart could

    __ __ __ __ __ __ __ __ __ for thirty minutes
    18 14 11 9 12 5 18 1 22
    without repeating himself.

8. We know Mozart's Symphony No. 41 in

    C Major (K.551) as the __ __ __ __ __ __ __
    17 6 11 18 7 22 9
    Symphony.

CLASSICAL CORNER: JOSEPH HAYDN   5-32

Use one of these answers, all having to do with numbers, to fill in the blanks below.

many   one   88   forty   eight   two   four   quartets

1. At the age of _____ Haydn was a choir boy in Vienna.

2. At a very early age Haydn picked up

   _____ sticks, pretending to have a violin and bow, and moved one across the other in perfect time to the music.

3. It was _____ of Haydn's dearest friends, Mozart, who began calling him "Papa Haydn," for his wit and good sense of humor.

4. Haydn developed _____ musical forms and for this he is known as the "father" of the symphony, sonata, and string quartet.

5. It was not until he was _____ that Haydn wrote works that we hear today.

6. Joseph Haydn, an Austrian composer, is best known for his symphonies and string

   _____.

7. Haydn's Symphony in G Major (No. ____) is known as the *Surprise* Symphony. The surprise is a loud chord after a quiet theme for strings and it is believed that Haydn used the chord to wake those up who dozed off to sleep.

8. Haydn wrote around eighty string quartets, for these _____ stringed instruments: two violins, viola, and cello.

CLASSICAL CORNER: LUDWIG van BEETHOVEN   5–33

Finish these statements about Beethoven by writing the missing words on the lines. Use the answers from the bottom of the page.

1. Beethoven had

   _____ .

2. Beethoven was

   _____ .

3. By the time Beethoven composed the *Eroica* Symphony, he was

   _____ .

4. It is remarkable that Beethoven, while stone-deaf, even conducted

   _____ .

5. Beethoven wrote five concertos for

   _____ .

6. "Moonlight," "Waldstein," "Appassionata," and "Hammerklavier," are all names of

   _____ .

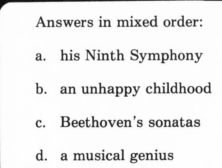

Answers in mixed order:

a. his Ninth Symphony

b. an unhappy childhood

c. Beethoven's sonatas

d. a musical genius

e. totally deaf

f. piano and orchestra

CLASSICAL CORNER: FREDERIC CHOPIN   5–34

Each of the statements below can be completed by using letters from the piano keyboard.

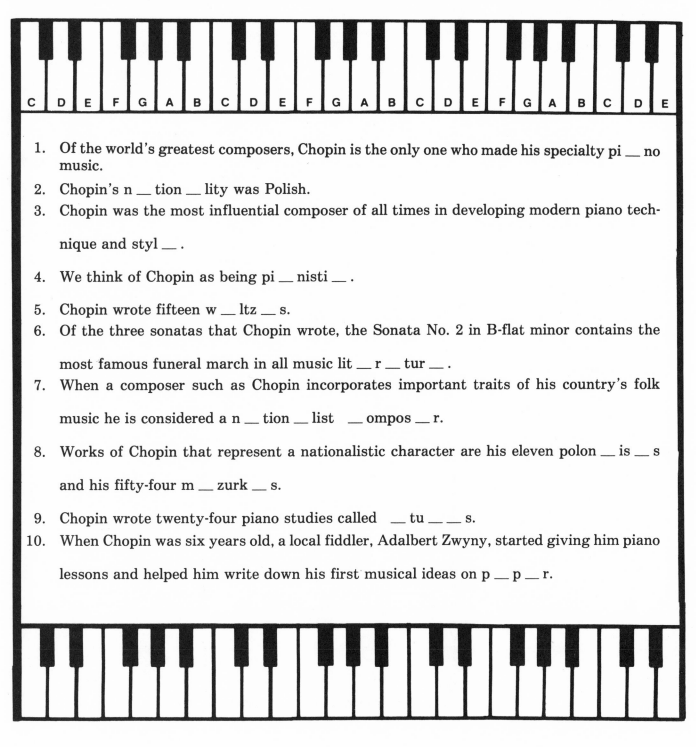

1. Of the world's greatest composers, Chopin is the only one who made his specialty pi __ no music.

2. Chopin's n __ tion __ lity was Polish.

3. Chopin was the most influential composer of all times in developing modern piano technique and styl __ .

4. We think of Chopin as being pi __ nisti __ .

5. Chopin wrote fifteen w __ ltz __ s.

6. Of the three sonatas that Chopin wrote, the Sonata No. 2 in B-flat minor contains the most famous funeral march in all music lit __ r __ tur __ .

7. When a composer such as Chopin incorporates important traits of his country's folk music he is considered a n __ tion __ list __ ompos __ r.

8. Works of Chopin that represent a nationalistic character are his eleven polon __ is __ s and his fifty-four m __ zurk __ s.

9. Chopin wrote twenty-four piano studies called __ tu __ __ s.

10. When Chopin was six years old, a local fiddler, Adalbert Zwyny, started giving him piano lessons and helped him write down his first musical ideas on p __ p __ r.

Activities for
RESEARCHING COMPOSERS

Name _____   Score _____

Date _____   Class _____

MAKING A LONG STORY SHORT   5–35

Choose a book or an encyclopedia that has information about a famous composer. List your source on the back of this sheet. After researching the information needed below, write your answers in the spaces.

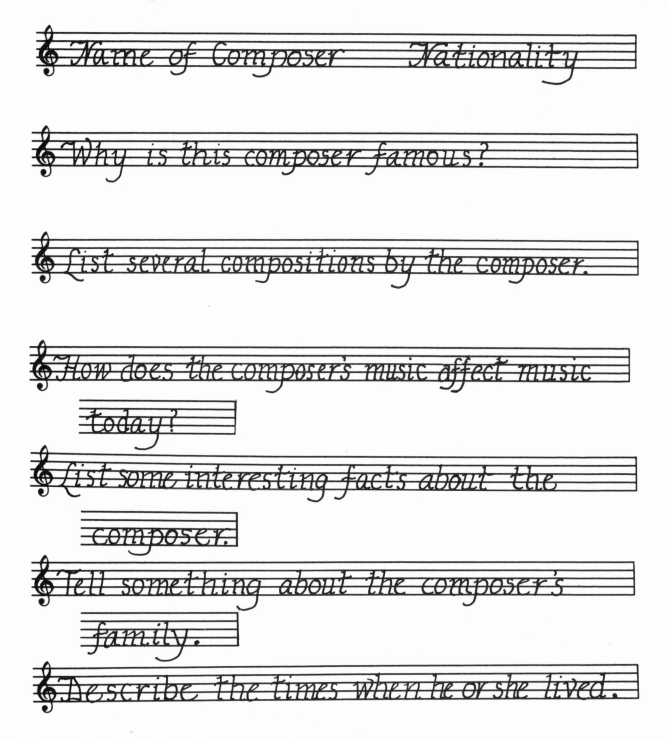

Name _____

Date _____

Score _____

Class _____

INSTRUMENT INVENTORY

1. What instruments did composers write for in the Baroque Period (1600–1750)?

2. What instruments do composers write for in our present day?

LET'S COMPARE BACH TO ROCK

1. Rock composers of today use many different instruments, devices, and sounds to produce music. How are the composers' sources of sound different today than they were during the time of Johann Sebastian Bach who lived from 1685 to 1750?

   _____

   _____

   _____

   _____

2. Composers during the time of Bach were limited in the types of music they wrote. Compare the forms of music composers chose to write in the Baroque Period to those of today.

   _____

   _____

   _____

3. For whom did Bach write his music?

   _____

4. What types of audiences do composers write for today?

   _____

   _____

WHAT TYPE OF AUDIENCE?   5–38

1. What types of audiences did composers write for in Mozart's time?

   _____

   _____

2. Name a composer who lived over one-hundred years ago and list one of his or her works.

   Name of Composer: _____

   Name of Composition: _____

3. What types of listening audiences do composers write for today?

   _____

   _____

4. Name a present-day composer and list one of his or her works.

   Name of Composer: _____

   Name of Composition: _____

Name _____

Date _____

Score _____

Class _____

DIAL A NAME

The numbers below stand for letters on a telephone dial. Each set stands for a composer's name. All you do is substitute the letters for the numbers. Work carefully because one number can stand for more than one letter. Use the title of one of their works as a clue to help you find their names.

1. "God Bless America   by _____
                                    478464   237546

2. "I Want to Hold Your Hand" by _____
                                    5646   536666

3. *The Sound of Music*   by _____
                                    7424273   7634377

4. *Stars and Stripes Forever* by _____
                                    5646   744547   76872

5. *Annie*   by _____
                                    2427537   7876873

6. *The Mikado*   by _____
                                    278487   78554826

PATRIOTIC PUZZLE

5-40

Match the lyricist with his or her song by writing the identifying letter on the blank. The first one is given as an example. When you are finished, the letters will spell a word that tells something about our country.

__R__ 1. Irving Berlin

_____ 2. Francis Scott Key

_____ 3. Woody Guthrie

_____ 4. Julia Ward Howe

_____ 5. Daniel D. Emmett

_____ 6. Samuel Francis Smith

_____ 7. George M. Cohan

_____ 8. Katharine Lee Bates

L.   "America"

C.   "America the Beautiful"

P.   "This Land Is Your Land"

E.   "The Star-Spangled Banner"

B.   "Dixie"

U.   "Battle Hymn of the Republic"

I.   "You're a Grand Old Flag"

R.   "God Bless America"

Use the outline below to design a shield using stars and stripes.

GET TO KNOW SOUSA

Use a library resource to answer these
questions about John Philip Sousa.

5–41

Let's honor the... "MARCH KING"

1. Who is John Philip Sousa? (Explain why he is famous, where he was born and lived, and give some interesting facts about his life.)

   _____

   _____

   _____

   _____

   _____

   _____

2. How many marches did Sousa write? _____

3. What is a march? _____

   _____

4. What special title does Sousa have? _____

5. Give the titles of three marches composed by Sousa.

   a. _____

   b. _____

   c. _____

Name _____   Score _____

Date _____   Class _____

LEARN ABOUT THE "KING OF RAGTIME"   5–42

Finish writing the sentences using the answers given at the bottom of the page.

1. Scott Joplin was _____

   _____ .

2. He was born _____

3. Before the age of seven _____

   _____ .

4. Joplin composed music that was _____

   _____ .

5. Joplin used traditional notation in published music ver-

   sions of his early music, _____

   _____ .

6. A composition of Joplin's that became a landmark in the

   history of American music was _____

   _____ .

7. Scott Joplin lived _____

   _____ .

a. from 1868–1917.
b. but he played it in syncopated style.
c. in Texas.
d. ahead of his time.
e. known as the "King of Ragtime."
f. Scott showed musical promise at the piano.
g. "The Maple Leaf Rag."

Name _____   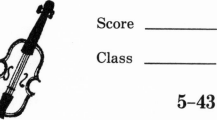   Score _____

Date _____   Class _____

MAKE A BIBLIOGRAPHY   5–43

Research the number of biographies about composers in your school and/or local library. Record the information below.

NAME OF COMPOSER	TITLE OF BOOK	PUBLISHER	AUTHOR	COPYRIGHT

RICHARD RODGERS, THE COMPOSER

Richard Rodgers wrote many musicals during his lifetime. Two of the musicals listed on this page were written by other composers. Draw cupid's arrow through those two.

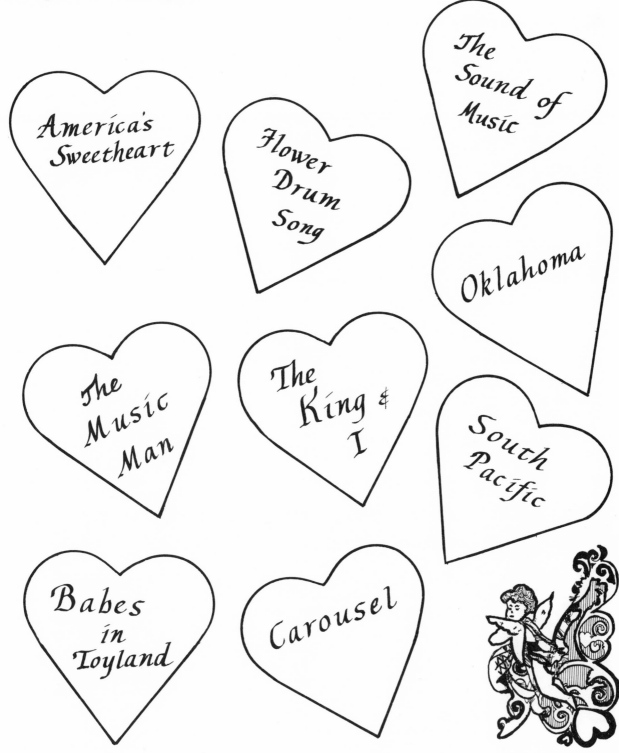

HELP THE HISTORIAN 5–45

Imagine that you have been asked by a music historian to help research American songs that played a part in American history. Complete your project by unscrambling the titles of these popular American songs that are still sung today.

1. ROF E'HS A LJOLY DOGO LOWLEF

   _____

2. PAPYH DRIYBATH

   _____

3. HO NASSUAN

   _____

4. LAUD NAGL NYSE

   _____

5. KIPS OT YM OLU

   _____

6. KANEYE DODELO

   _____

7. EHT LOWLEY SORE FO XASET

   _____

8. HE'SLL BE MONIC' 'NOURD HET TOUNMAIN

   _____

9. SWIGN WOL, WESET TRIOACH

   _____

10. HO NEHW HET NAISTS OG CHARMING NI

   _____

Name _____   Score _____

Date _____   Class _____

FINISH THE TITLE   5-46

Listed here are the names of composers who are well-known for their operettas, musicals, or popular music. Use each of the twenty-six letters of the alphabet to complete these song titles and the secret message below. Place one letter on each space. (Cross out each letter as you use it.)

A   B   C   D   E   F   G   H   I   J   K   L   M

N   O   P   Q   R   S   T   U   V   W   X   Y   Z

1. Jerry Bock
"Fiddl __ r on the Ro __ f"

2. Cole Porter
"__ ust One of Those Things"

3. George Cohan
"Yo __ 're A __ rand Old __ lag"

4. Gus Edwards
"Schoo __ __ ays"

5. Ferdé Grofé
"Gr __ nd Can __ on Suite"

6. Hoagy Carmichael
" __ tardust"

7. Al Hoffman
"Ma __ r __ y Doats"

8. Henry Mancini
"Pin __ __ ant __ er"

9. James Van Heusen
"S __ inging on a Sta __ "

10. Albert Von Tilzer
" __ ake Me Out to the __ allga __ e"

11. Meredith Willson
"The Musi __ Ma __ "

Secret message: Be e __ tra __ uiet while doing this acti __ ity!

WHO, WHAT, AND WHEN?   5–47

Listed below are the birthdates of seven composers from the Romantic period in history, and a work by the composer. Each was born the same year another important event took place. Match the event printed inside the flying machine with the composer's birthdate by writing the event on the blank. Use a reference book if necessary.

1. 1859   Birth of Victor Herbert
    The Red Mill (operetta) _____

2. 1861   Birth of MacDowell
    Woodland Sketches (piano pieces) _____

3. 1865   Birth of Sibelius
    Finlandia (tone poem for orchestra) _____

4. 1876   Birth of Falla
    El Amor Brujo (ballet/suite) _____

5. 1879   Birth of Respighi
    The Pines of Rome (orchestral suite) _____

6. 1895   Birth of Hindemith
    Mathis der Maler (opera/symphony) _____

7. 1898   Birth of Gershwin
    Porgy and Bess (blues folk opera) _____

Roentgen . . . X-ray
Beginning of Civil War
Edison . . . Light bulb
Spanish-American War
End of Civil War
Bell . . . Telephone
Darwin . . . *The Origin
of Species*

MATCH THE PUZZLE PIECES   5-48

Each of the composers listed has written a group of works including operettas, musicals, and popular music. The titles of the works are given below in puzzle pieces. Match the composer with the works by writing the name of the composer on the blank puzzle piece.

Irving Berlin
John Philip Sousa
Charles Strouse
Burt Bacharach
Arthur Sullivan
Richard Rodgers

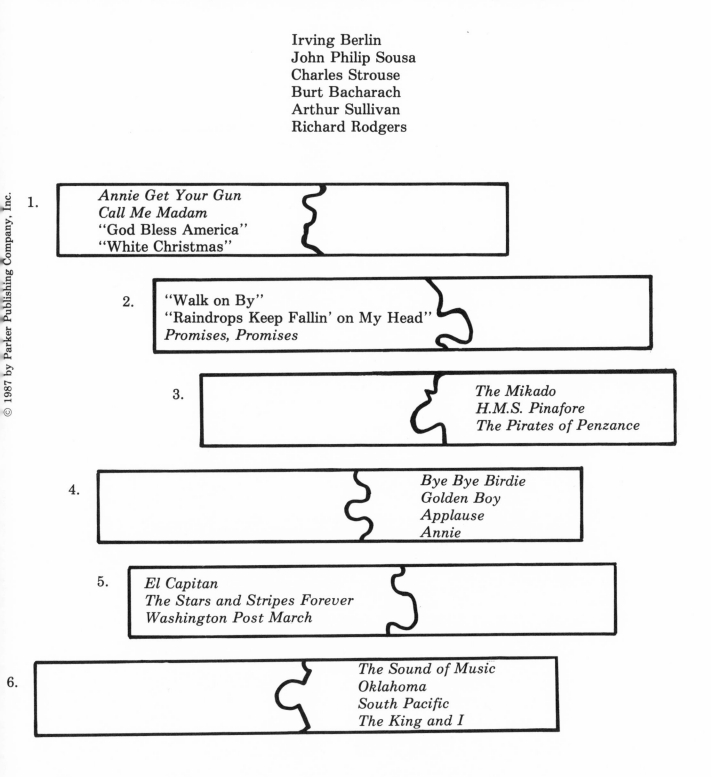

1. *Annie Get Your Gun*
Call Me Madam
"God Bless America"
"White Christmas"

2. "Walk on By"
"Raindrops Keep Fallin' on My Head"
Promises, Promises

3. *The Mikado*
H.M.S. Pinafore
The Pirates of Penzance

4. *Bye Bye Birdie*
Golden Boy
Applause
Annie

5. *El Capitan*
The Stars and Stripes Forever
Washington Post March

6. *The Sound of Music*
Oklahoma
South Pacific
The King and I

WHEN DID THEY COMPOSE?   5-49

Write the name of the period in music history in which each of the following groups of composers belong:

Igor Stravinsky (Russian)
Aaron Copland (American)
1. _____ Jean Berger (American)
Samuel Barber (American)

Georg Philipp Telemann (German)
Johann Sebastian Bach (German)
2. _____ Domenico Scarlatti (Italian)
George Frederick Handel (German)

Joseph Haydn (Austrian)
Muzio Clementi (Italian)
3. _____ Wolfgang Amadeus Mozart (German)
Ludwig van Beethoven (German)

Felix Mendelssohn (German)
Franz Liszt (Hungarian)
4. _____ Johannes Brahms (German)
Peter Ilich Tchaikovsky (Russian)

BAROQUE PERIOD (1600–1750)
CLASSICAL PERIOD (1750–1800)
ROMANTIC PERIOD (1800–1900)
CONTEMPORARY PERIOD (1900–Present)

FINISH THE TIME LINE

On the time line, write in the musical highlights between the literary accomplishments that occurred during the given dates. Choose your answers from the bottom of the page. Use a reference book if necessary.

1386	Chaucer: *The Canterbury Tales*
1554	1. _____
1594	Shakespeare: *Romeo and Juliet*
1669	2. _____
1719	Defoe: *Robinson Crusoe*
1741	3. _____
1820	Scott: *Ivanhoe*
1846	4. _____
1878	Hardy: *Return of the Native*
1900	5. _____
1916	Sandburg: *Chicago Poems*
1943	6. _____
1952	Hemingway: *The Old Man and the Sea*
1971	7. _____
1981	Henley: *Crimes of the Heart*
1984	8. _____

Musical Highlights
(Listed in mixed order)

Bartók: Concerto for Orchestra

Paris Opera Established by Lully

Palestrina: *First Book of Masses*

Mendelssohn: *Elijah*

Handel: *Messiah*

Webber-Rice's Musical: *Jesus Christ Superstar*

Philadelphia Symphony Orchestra Founded

Video Music on TV Evolves: Michael Jackson's "Beat It"

Answer Key
for *Great Composers and Their Music*

5-1 DESIGNER'S WORKSHOP

Drawings will vary.

5-2 MY FAVORITE SONG IS . . .

Drawings will vary.

5-3 AN AUTHENTIC PORTRAIT

Drawings will vary.

5-4 SHOW AND TELL

Drawings will vary.

5-5 PETER AND THE WOLF

1. Peter
2. Bird
3. Duck
4. Cat
5. Wolf
6. Grandfather
7. Hunters

5-6 CARNIVAL OF THE ANIMALS

1. Royal March of the Lion
2. Hens and Roosters
3. Mules
4. Turtles
5. Elephant
6. Kangaroos
7. Aquarium
8. Donkeys
9. Cuckoo (bird)
10. Aviary
11. Pianist
12. Fossils
13. Swan
14. Finale (lion, donkeys, hens and roosters, kangaroos, and "hee-haws")

5-7 THE NUTCRACKER SUITE

Drawings will vary.

5-8 SCHEHERAZADE

Drawings will vary.

5-9 THE SORCERER'S APPRENTICE

Drawings will vary.

5-10 PICTURES AT AN EXHIBITION

Drawings will vary. A selection for listening might be "The Ballet of the Unhatched Chickens."

5-11 A DAY IN THE LIFE OF . . .

Answers will vary.

5-12 WRITE A FEATURE STORY

Answers will vary.

5-13 A COMPOSER'S CHOICE

Answers will vary, but some suggested answers are:

1. A composer may begin by first writing the lyrics or the melody.
2. Examples are classical, opera, ballet, blues, rock, gospel, country, commercials, movie soundtracks.
3. Any six instruments are acceptable.
4. Examples are concert audience, television viewers, church parishioners, radio listeners, dancers.

5-14 MY FAVORITE COMPOSER TODAY IS . . .

Answers will vary.

5-15 GETTING ACQUAINTED

Answers will vary.

5-16 A PERSONAL HISTORY OF . . .

Answers will vary.

5-17 CURTAIN CALL

1. Bach
2. Beethoven
3. Brahms
4. Chopin
5. Debussy
6. Handel
7. Haydn
8. Hindemith
9. Liszt
10. Milhaud
11. Mozart
12. Mussorgsky
13. Prokofiev
14. Saint-Saëns
15. Schubert
16. Schumann
17. Shostakovich
18. Sibelius
19. Sousa
20. Tchaikovsky

5-18 DECODE WITH VOWELS

Activity sheet is self-checking.

5-19 WHAT'S THEIR NATIONALITY?

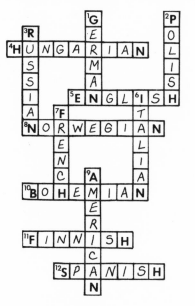

5–20   WHO WROTE THE OPERA?

5–21   CRAZY CLUES

This activity sheet is self-checking.

5–22   COMPOSER TRIVIA

This activity sheet is self-checking.

5–23   DANCE DATA

This activity sheet is self-checking.

5–24 NAME THE OTHER TITLE

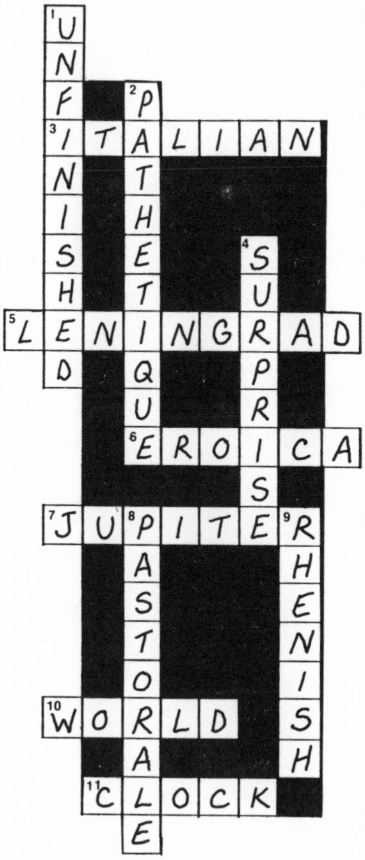
1 UNFINISHED
2 PATHETIQUE
3 ITALIAN
4 SURPRISE
5 LENINGRAD
6 EROICA
7 JUPITER
8 PASTORALE
9 RHENISH
10 WORLD
11 CLOCK

5–25 WHO WROTE IT?

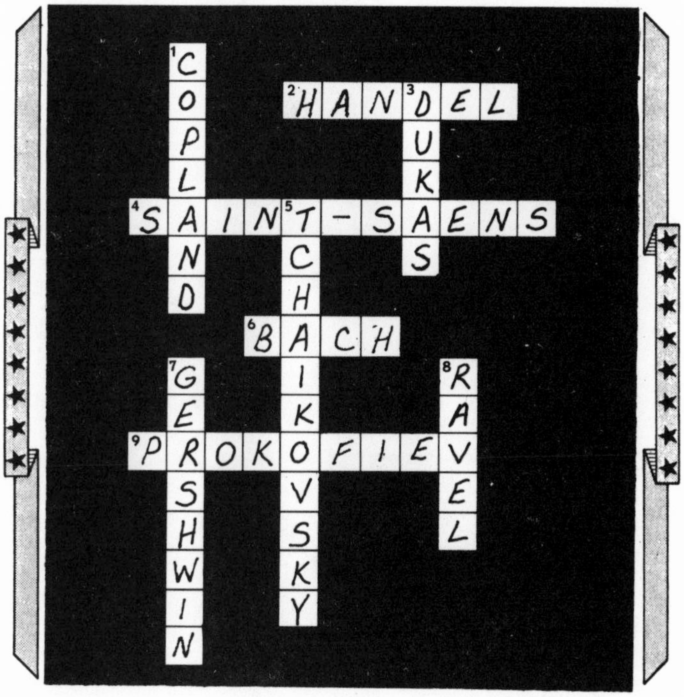
1 COPLAND
2 HANDEL
3 DUKAS
4 SAINT-SAENS
5 TCHAIKOVSKY
6 BACH
7 GERSHWIN
8 RAVEL
9 PROKOFIEV

5-26 COMPLETE THE TITLE

5-27 IDENTIFY THE SYMPHONY

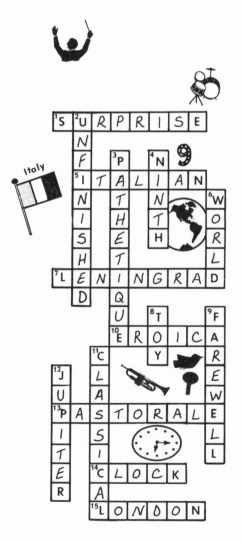

5-28 REVEAL THE COMPOSER

5-29 CLASSICAL CORNER: JOHANN SEBASTIAN BACH

1. composer
2. volumes
3. eyesight
4. church
5. Matthew

6. voice
7. piano
8. organ
9. orchestra
10. Period

5-30 CLASSICAL CORNER: GEORGE FREDERICK HANDEL

This activity is self-checking.

5-31 CLASSICAL CORNER: WOLFGANG AMADEUS MOZART

The code goes from A = 26 to Z = 1.

1. genius
2. minuets
3. symphony
4. Marriage

5. memory
6. tones
7. improvise
8. Jupiter

5-32 CLASSICAL CORNER: JOSEPH HAYDN

1. eight
2. two
3. one
4. many

5. forty
6. quartets
7. 88
8. four

5-33 CLASSICAL CORNER: LUDWIG VAN BEETHOVEN

1. b   4. a
2. d   5. f
3. e   6. c

5-34 CLASSICAL CORNER: FREDERIC CHOPIN

1. piano   6. literature
2. nationality   7. nationalist composer
3. style   8. polonaises, mazurkas
4. pianistic   9. etudes
5. waltzes   10. paper

5-35 MAKING A LONG STORY SHORT

Answers will vary.

5-36 INSTRUMENT INVENTORY

Answers will vary. Suggested answers for # 1 are: clavier, clavichord, harpsichord, organ, string quartet (first and second violin, viola, and cello), lute, recorder, oboe, trumpets, flutes, timpani, and various brass instruments.

5-37 LET'S COMPARE BACH TO ROCK

Answers will vary, but suggested answers are:

1. Composers during the time of Bach were more restricted than the composers of today. Today's composers use unlimited sources of sounds for music such as synthesizers, electronic devices, and computers.
2. During Bach's time, composers generally wrote in the following categories: (a) choral music: oratorios, masses, cantatas; (b) orchestra music: concertos, suites; (c) piano music: music for the clavier, suites; (d) chamber music: sonatas; and (e) organ music: preludes, fugues, chorales. For the types of music composers write for today, answers will vary.
3. the church
4. Answers will vary.

5-38 WHAT TYPE OF AUDIENCE?

1. theater, royalty, church, home
2-6. Answers will vary.

5-39 DIAL A NAME

1. Irving Berlin   4. John Philip Sousa
2. John Lennon   5. Charles Strouse
3. Richard Rodgers   6. Arthur Sullivan

5-40 PATRIOTIC PUZZLE

The answers will spell out REPUBLIC.

5-41 GET TO KNOW SOUSA

1. Suggested answer: John Philip Sousa was a great composer. The first major event in his life was at the age of 13 when his father decided to enlist him in the United States Marine Band. During that time, he learned what he needed to know to organize his own band. In 1892, he did just that. Sousa also became a cultural statesman with worldwide fame.

2. 103
3. A march is a musical composition to accompany a band or troop while marching (walking). A march is usually written in 2/4 or 6/8 meter.
4. March King
5. Suggested answers:

   Stars and Stripes Forever (his most famous march)

   Semper Fidelis

   The Thunderer

   Washington Post

   El Capitan

5-42 LEARN ABOUT THE "KING OF RAGTIME"

1. e
2. c
3. f
4. d

5. b
6. g
7. a

5-43 MAKE A BIBLIOGRPAHY

Bibliographies will differ.

5-44 RICHARD RODGERS, THE COMPOSER

The Music Man (written by Meredith Willson)

Babes in Toyland (written by Victor Herbert)

5-45 HELP THE HISTORIAN

1. "For He's a Jolly Good Fellow"
2. "Happy Birthday"
3. "Oh Susanna"
4. "Auld Lang Syne"
5. "Skip to My Lou"

6. "Yankee Doodle"
7. "The Yellow Rose of Texas"
8. "She'll Be Comin' 'Round the Mountain"
9. "Swing Low, Sweet Chariot"
10. "Oh When the Saints Go Marching In"

5-46 FINISH THE TITLE

1. *Fiddler on the Roof*
2. "Just One of Those Things"
3. "You're a Grand Old Flag"
4. "School Days"
5. *Grand Canyon Suite*
6. "Stardust"

7. "Mairzy Doats"
8. "Pink Panther"
9. "Swinging on a Star"
10. "Take Me Out to the Ballgame"
11. *The Music Man*

5-47 WHO, WHAT, AND WHEN?

1. Darwin . . . *The Origin of Species*
2. Beginning of Civil War
3. End of Civil War
4. Bell . . . Telephone

5. Edison . . . Light bulb
6. Roentgen . . . X-ray
7. Spanish-American War

5-48 MATCH THE PUZZLE PIECES

1. Irving Berlin
2. Burt Bacharach
3. Arthur Sullivan
4. Charles Strouse
5. John Philip Sousa
6. Richard Rodgers

5-49 WHEN DID THEY COMPOSE?

1. Contemporary Period (1900–Present)
2. Baroque Period (1600–1750)
3. Classical Period (1750–1800)
4. Romantic Period (1800–1900)

5-50 FINISH THE TIME LINE

1. Palestrina: *First Book of Masses*
2. Paris Opera Established by Lully
3. Handel: *Messiah*
4. Mendelssohn: *Elijah*
5. Philadelphia Symphony Orchestra Founded
6. Bartók: Concerto for Orchestra
7. Webber-Rice's Musical: *Jesus Christ Superstar*
8. Video Music on TV Evolves: Michael Jackson's "Beat It"

Progress Chart for
Great Composers and Their Music

Use this chart to keep a record of activities completed for each class. List your classes (or students) in the given spaces at the right. As each activity is completed for a class, mark an "X" in the appropriate column.

Activity Number/Title		Skill Involved				
Creative Drawing						
5-1	DESIGNER'S WORKSHOP	Drawing a portrait or caricature of a composer and writing a slogan				
5-2	MY FAVORITE SONG IS . . .	Drawing a picture describing a favorite song with the composer's name				
5-3	AN AUTHENTIC PORTRAIT	Sketching a picture of a favorite composer				
5-4	SHOW AND TELL	Designing a record album jacket for a favorite song				
5-5	PETER AND THE WOLF	Drawing characters to match the sounds of the instruments				
5-6	CARNIVAL OF THE ANIMALS	Drawing animals to match the sounds of instruments				
5-7	THE NUTCRACKER SUITE	Illustrating the handsome prince				
5-8	SCHEHERAZADE	Drawing the Sultan or Sultana Scheherazade				
5-9	THE SORCERER'S APPRENTICE	Drawing one of the scenes from this musical story				
5-10	PICTURES AT AN EXHIBITION	Drawing a favorite picture from this symphonic work				
Creative Writing						
5-11	A DAY IN THE LIFE OF . . .	Writing about a typical day in the life of a favorite composer				
5-12	WRITE A FEATURE STORY	Writing a feature story for the school newspaper about a composer				

Activity Number/Title		Skill Involved				
5-13	A COMPOSER'S CHOICE	Answering questions about how a composer creates, makes choices, and so on				
5-14	MY FAVORITE COMPOSER TODAY IS . . .	Writing an article about a favorite composer				
5-15	GETTING ACQUAINTED	Gathering information about a composer				
5-16	A PERSONAL HISTORY OF . . .	Using a guideline to write a personal history of a composer				

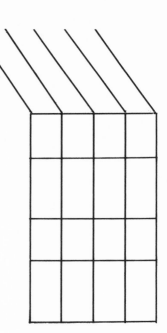

Learning About the Masters and Their Works

5-17	CURTAIN CALL	Pronouncing and spelling names correctly of famous composers				
5-18	DECODE WITH VOWELS	Completing the titles of works by national composers using vowels				
5-19	WHAT'S THEIR NATIONALITY?	Writing nationalities of the masters in a crossword puzzle				
5-20	WHO WROTE THE OPERA?	Naming composers of famous operas				
5-21	CRAZY CLUES	Using crazy clues to name famous compositions				
5-22	COMPOSER TRIVIA	Reading statements about composers to guess their names				
5-23	DANCE DATA	Unscrambling and decoding names of composers who wrote famous dances				
5-24	NAME THE OTHER TITLE	Naming another title for a symphonic work				
5-25	WHO WROTE IT?	Naming famous composers from their works				
5-26	COMPLETE THE TITLE	Finishing titles of famous works by the masters				
5-27	IDENTIFY THE SYMPHONY	Identifying symphonies by clues about composers				
5-28	REVEAL THE COMPOSER	Identifying composers by clues				

Activity Number/Title	Skill Involved					

A Closer Look at Some Famous Classical Composers

5-29	CLASSICAL CORNER: JOHANN SEBASTIAN BACH	Using letter names of organ pedals to complete statements about Bach				
5-30	CLASSICAL CORNER: GEORGE FREDERICK HANDEL	Completing missing words in statements about Handel				
5-31	CLASSICAL CORNER: WOLFGANG AMADEUS MOZART	Decoding words to finish facts about Mozart				
5-32	CLASSICAL CORNER: JOSEPH HAYDN	Using numbers to complete facts about Haydn				
5-33	CLASSICAL CORNER: LUDWIG VAN BEETHOVEN	Choosing an answer to finish each statement about Beethoven				
5-34	CLASSICAL CORNER: FREDERIC CHOPIN	Using letters from the keyboard to finish statements about Chopin				

Enrichment Activities for Researching Composers

5-35	MAKING A LONG STORY SHORT	Researching certain information about a famous composer				
5-36	INSTRUMENT INVENTORY	Comparing instruments that composers wrote for during the Baroque Period and today				
5-37	LET'S COMPARE BACH TO ROCK	Answering questions to compare the music of Bach to today's rock music				
5-38	WHAT TYPE OF AUDIENCE?	Comparing composers of Mozart's time to those of today				
5-39	DIAL A NAME	Using the titles of popular songs and musicals to decode names of composers				
5-40	PATRIOTIC PUZZLE	Matching the lyricist with his or her well-known patriotic song				
5-41	GET TO KNOW SOUSA	Using a library resource to answer questions about John Philip Sousa				
5-42	LEARN ABOUT THE "KING OF RAGTIME"	Completing facts about Scott Joplin				

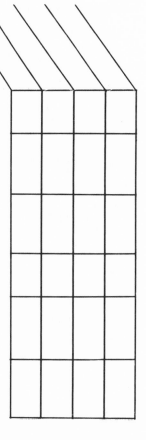

Activity Number/Title		Skill Involved	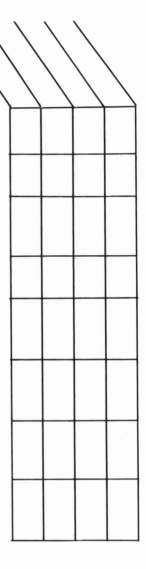
5-43	MAKE A BIBLIOGRAPHY	Researching biographies of composers in the school or local library	
5-44	RICHARD RODGERS, THE COMPOSER	Identifying musicals of Rodgers	
5-45	HELP THE HISTORIAN	Unscrambling titles of popular American songs throughout history	
5-46	FINISH THE TITLE	Completing song titles of well-known composers	
5-47	WHO, WHAT, AND WHEN?	Matching events in history to birthdates of famous composers	
5-48	MATCH THE PUZZLE PIECES	Matching composers to their operettas, musicals, or pop music	
5-49	WHEN DID THEY COMPOSE?	Matching dates in history with names of famous composers	
5-50	FINISH THE TIME LINE	Matching dates of musical highlights with literary achievements	

Great Composers and Their Music

Bach	Mendelssohn
Barber	Menotti
Bartók	Milhaud
Beethoven	Mozart
Bernstein	Mussorgsky
Bizet	Offenbach
Bock	Prokofiev
Brahms	Puccini
Chopin	Ravel
Copland	Respighi
Debussy	Rimsky-Korsakov
Dukas	Rodgers
Dvořák	Romberg
Elgar	Rossini
Flotow	Saint-Saëns
Gershwin	Schubert
Granados	Schumann
Grieg	Shostakovich
Grofé	Sibelius
Handel	Smetana
Haydn	Sousa
Hindemith	Sullivan
Humperdinck	Tchaikovsky
Joplin	Vaughan Williams
Lehar	Verdi
Liszt	Wagner
Mahler	

Name _____

Date _____

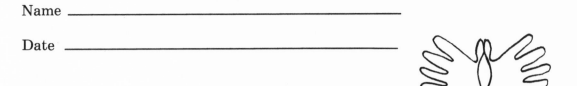

Craft Project
for *Great Composers*
and Their Music

"THE WORLD OF COMPOSING" SCRAPBOOK

Objective: This loose-leaf scrapbook can be used in various ways. Students will enjoy this activity as a natural outgrowth of interests already started. It can be used at any time when this unit is being studied to add an incentive for additional learning. Making the scrapbook contributes to thinking, creative ability, appreciation for good music, development of good work habits and music skills, as well as independent study.

Materials Needed:

- 18″ × 24″ colored construction paper
- Three-hole notebook paper
- Hole puncher
- Scissors
- Yarn, shoelace, heavy string, or ribbon
- Crayons, markers, or colored pencils
- *Optional:* Music or artwork to mount on cover
- *Optional:* Glue

Construction Directions:

1. Fold the 18″ × 24″ sheet of construction paper in half to form a 9″ × 12″ cover. While the paper is folded, place a sheet of three-hole notebook paper on the top as a guide to punch the holes. Trace around the holes and then punch three holes along the folded edge.

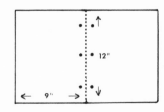

2. Line up all the notebook paper inside the cover. Thread a piece of yarn through the holes as shown in the illustration, and tie the loose ends in a bow. When you need to add more pages to the scrapbook just untie the yarn and place them where needed.

3. Write "The World of Composing" on the front cover along with your name. Use one of your own original ideas for a cover design or select one of the following suggestions:

   a. Draw a portrait of a composer of your choice.

   b. Cut out a silhouette of a composer you have sketched and glue it to the cover.

   c. Use a music-related art project, such as drawing to music. Cut out a portion of the illustration and mount it on the cover.

   d. Cut out the frame of a completed activity relating to composing and mount it to the front cover.

   e. Cut out or tear music symbols, such as notes, to decorate the cover.

   f. Draw wavy staff lines and draw notes on the staff or write the scrapbook's title on the staff.

Uses: The following ideas are only suggestions and starting points for compiling "The World of Composing" scrapbook. Allow students to be creative in the types of information about composing they wish to include.

1. An original poem or a personal history of a composer.

2. A collection of newspaper clippings, magazine articles, or pictures about a composer; possibly include reviews and advertising about a musical event coming to your area involving a certain composer

3. Book reports on stories about composers or on biographies

4. Original artwork—drawings of composers, drawings typifying the time period in which the composer lived, drawing of composer's national flag, drawing or painting to music, and so on

5. Review of a concert or performance recently attended

6. Notes taken about composers from lectures, discussions, special seminars, films, guest performers, movies, television specials

7. Storage for student work from this unit or one of the other units where the activity relates to composing or composers

8. A reference page noting sources of information used

Incentive Badges

To the teacher: Cut apart badges and keep in a handy 3″ × 5″ file box along with tape. Encourage students to write their names and the date on the backs of their badges and to wear them.

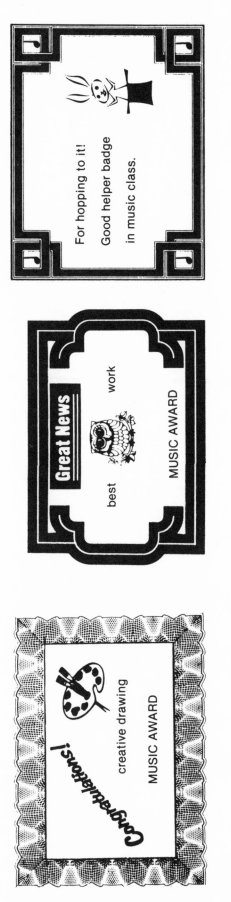
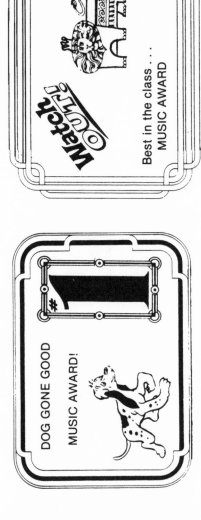

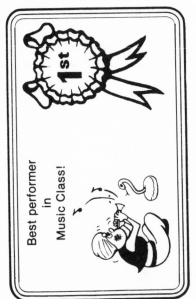

MUSIC SHARE-A-GRAM

TO: _____ ·DATE _____
(Parent's Name)

FROM: _____ SCHOOL _____
(Classroom Music Teacher)

RE: _____ CLASS _____
(Student's Name)

To help you recognize your child's success in music class or any area that needs attention the following observation(s) has/have been made.

	Exceptional	Satisfactory	Unsatisfactory
Shows musical aptitude			
Shows creativity			
Shows talent			
Shows initiative			
Self-concept in music class			
Fairness in dealing with classmates			
Self-direction			
Care of instrument and equipment			
Reaction to constructive criticism			
Observes music class rules			
Starts and completes work on time			
Generally follows directions			

over for comments ▶

- -

RETURN-A-GRAM

TO: _____ DATE _____
(Classroom Music Teacher)

FROM: _____ SCHOOL _____
(Parent's Name)

RE: _____ CLASS _____
(Student's Name)

Please write your comments or questions on the back and return. If you want to be called for a parent-teacher conference, indicate below.

_____ Class _____ Year _____

(Student's Name)

STUDENT RECORD PROFILE CHART

Select the appropriate data in parentheses for each category, i, ii, iii, and iv, and record the information in the chart below as shown in the example.

i.—Unit Number for *Music Curriculum Activities Library* (1, 2, 3, 4, 5, 6, 7)

ii.—Date (Day/Month)

iii.—Semester (1, 2, 3, 4) or Summer School: Session 1 (S1), Session 2 (S2)

iv.—Score: Select one of the three grading systems, a., b., or c., that applies to your school progress report and/or applies to the specific activity.

a.

(O)	= Outstanding
(G)	= Good
(S)	= Satisfactory
(NI)	= Needs Improvement
(U)	= Unsatisfactory
(I)	= Incomplete
(—)	= Absent

b.

(A)	= 93–100 [percentage score]
(B)	= 85–92
(C)	= 75–84
(D)	= 70–74
(F)	= 0–69
(I)	= Incomplete
(—)	= Absent

c. (R/P):

R	= Correct number of responses.
P	= Possible correct number of responses.
(I)	= Incomplete
(—)	= Absent

i	ii											
iii	iv											

Student's Name —————————— Class ——— Year ———

MUSIC SELF-IMPROVEMENT CHART (for student use)

a. On the back of this chart write your goal(s) for music class at the beginning of each semester.
b. On a separate sheet record the date and each new music skill you have acquired during the semester.

c. MUSIC SHARE-A-GRAM (date sent to parent)

d. RETURN-A-GRAM (date returned to teacher)

e. MUSIC AWARD BADGES (date and type rec'd)

1.
2.
3.

f. SPECIAL MUSIC RECOGNITION (date and type rec'd)

1.
2.
3.

g. SPECIAL MUSIC EVENT ATTENDANCE RECORD (date and name of special performance, recital, rehearsal, concert, field trip, film, workshop, seminar, institute, etc.)

1.
2.
3.
4.

h. ABOVE AND BEYOND: Extra Credit Projects (date and name of book report, classroom performance, construction of hand-made instrument, report on special music performance on TV, etc.)

1.
2.
3.
4.

i. PROGRESS REPORT/REPORT CARD RECORD (semester and grade received)

1.
2.
3.
4.

j. MUSIC SIGN-OUT RECORD (name of instrument, music, book or equipment with sign-out date and due date)

1.
2.
3.
4.
5.
6.
7.
8.
9.
10.

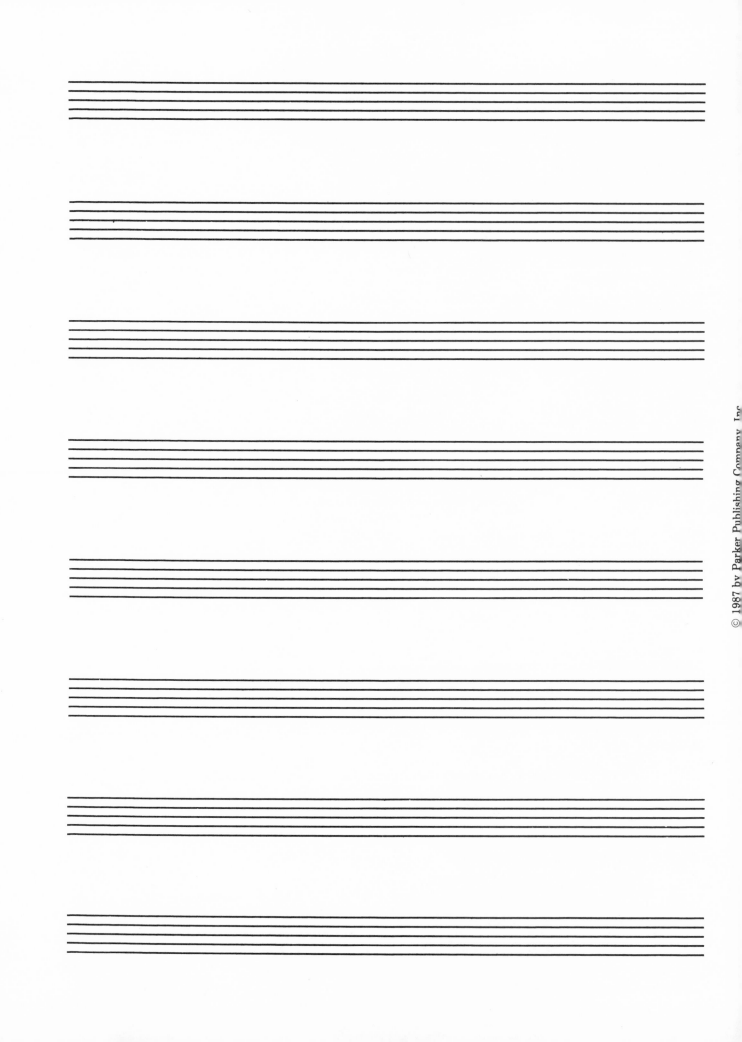

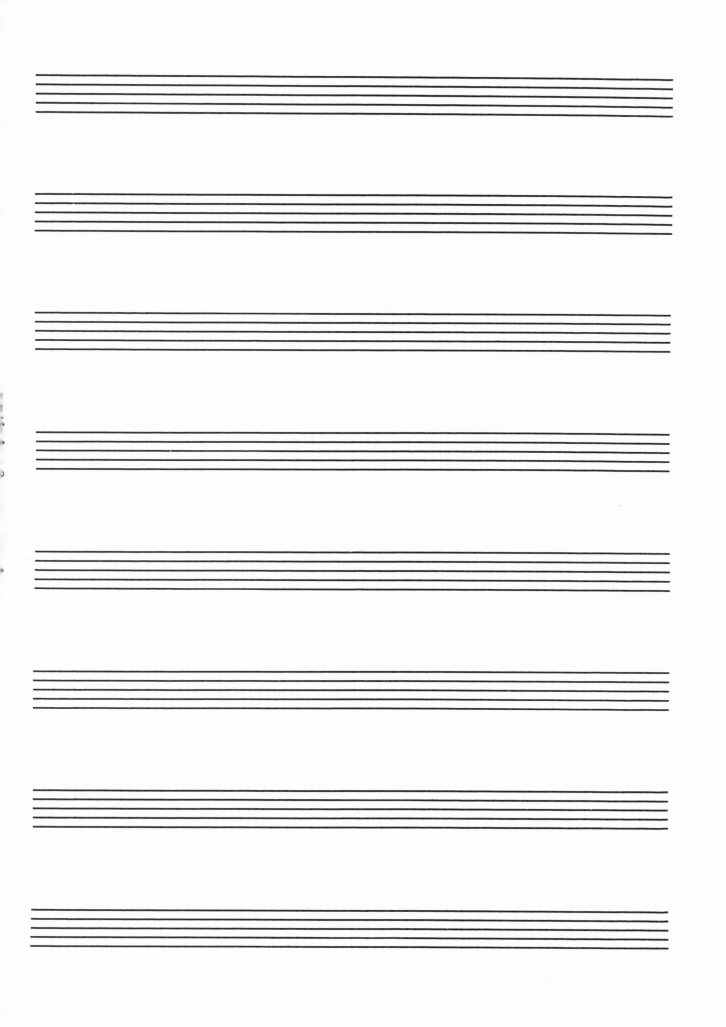

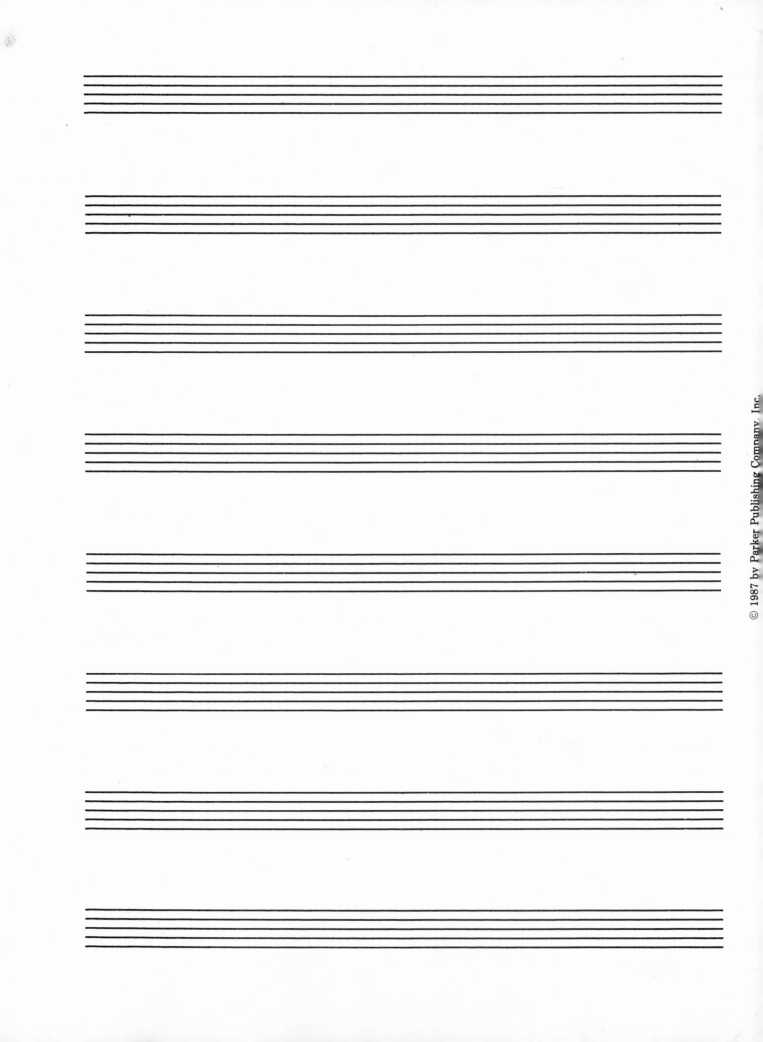